Projects on "Innovation in SMEs" in the Baltic Sea Region

- Experiences and Perspectives

Published by

Baltic Sea Academy e.V.
Dr Max Hogefoster
Blankeneser Landstrasse 7,
22587 Hamburg, Germany

Website of the cluster: **www.bsr-innovation.eu**

Editorial Correspondence: editor@baltic-sea-academy.eu

Printed by BoD-Books on Demand, Norderstedt, Germany

ISBN 9783732294459

All projects participating in this cluster were part-financed by the European Union (European Development Fund and European Neighbourhood and Partnership Instrument). This publication does not necessarily reflect the opinion of the Programme or the European Commission.

We are very grateful to the European Commission for the financial support and also to the Joint Technical Secretariat of the INTERREG IVB Programme for the support and advice.

Content

1. Part : 13 Projects in a nutshell

2. Part: Survey 2013

3. Part: Action Fields

Foreword

Innovative companies are the key for a competitive Baltic Sea Region. Objective of this publication is to inform about successful project and provide some input for possible future projects, that will further boost the innovation capacities of the small and medium-sized enterprises (SMEs).

SMEs are the blood cells of the Baltic Sea Region. However, to keep on nurturing economic growth and welfare in the Baltic Sea Region, the SMEs need support in the most important task of a knowledge society: creating innovation.

Over 99% of all enterprises in the region are SMEs, most of them micro companies with less than 5 employees. SMEs provide up to 80% of all jobs; in fact SMEs carried Europe through the financial crisis between 2008 and 2011. Compared to large firms and major industries', employment in SMEs proved to be more resilient[1].

Between 2002 and 2010 about 85% of net new jobs were created by small and medium sized enterprises, most patents registered by these firms, thus establishing it the most significant growth driver.

Due to relative high tax and social costs in the Baltic Sea Region, the local companies cannot compete with other countries in terms of prices, but only with high quality products and services. To stay competitive on the global market versus low labour cost countries like China, the regional enterprises must create products and services of high quality and exploit their full innovation potential.

In 2012 the Baltic Sea Region Programme initiated the cluster "**Innovation in SMEs**", starting with ten projects that focused their work on this important topic. During 2013 three additional projects joined the initiative. Most projects are flagship

---

[1] A recovery on the horizon, Annual report on European SMEs 2012/2013 for the European Commission, available from http://ec.europa.eu/enterprise/policies/sme/facts-figures-analysis/performance-review/files/supporting-documents/2013/annual-report-smes-2013_en.pdf

projects within the EU Strategy for the Baltic Sea region, namely in Priority SME Networks, Innovation and Education.

This publications can provide guidance to the political stakeholders and programming bodies about possible new or widened topics when promoting innovation in SMEs.

Altogether, the projects consist of more than 210 organisations in the Baltic Sea Region. Business organisations, chambers, universities, business incubators, R&D Institutions and administrations teamed up to support the small and medium sized enterprises in the Baltic Sea Region. Most projects ran for a period of three years, between 2008 and 2014.

In the first part of this publication the projects are summarized and share some of their results and lessons learned.

The second part highlights the most significant the results of a comprehensive survey that was conducted from spring to fall 2013. This survey provides a good overview on the topic, the current situation in the region and the future demands.

Based on the results of this survey and the work of the projects, a summary is provided, focusing on the most important needs of small and medium sized enterprises in the Baltic Sea Region in the near future. Tree action fields have been identified this way.

If those action fields are considered in future programmes and projects, the SMEs in the Baltic Sea Region can greatly contribute to make this one of the most innovative regions in the world again.

Hanse-Parlament
February 2014

1. Part: 13 projects in a nutshell

1 I Baltic Supply[2]

1. Project in a nutshell

The overall objective of BalticSupply was to strengthen the small and medium-sized supply industry in the Baltic Sea Region. It focused on the three regional key sectors 1) maritime industries, 2) energy, and 3) health, and created supply clusters for each sector, offering online and offline services for SMEs to support innovations and market development. Uniquely, BalticSupply closely cooperated with the sister project North Sea Supply Connect. Both projects joined forces to set up a European Business Support Network offering support to SMEs offline and online. The online platform is still growing and active after project end, hosted and administrated by the Hanse-Parlament.

2. Project partners

BalticSupply is led by the Ministry of Economic Affairs, Labour and Ports of the Free Hanseatic City of Bremen. The 15 project partners range from public authorities to regional development agencies, business development organisations as well as universities and research organisations.

3. Aims of the project

National markets in the Baltic Sea Region often are too small, and additionally SMEs are facing problems entering European supply markets, e.g. because of foreign laws and standards, lack of direct access to tenders or project partners. These circumstances cause competitive disadvantages for SMEs and the entire Baltic Sea Region in general.

BalticSupply aimed to generate new business opportunities for SMEs. The supply clusters were created to improve SMEs' innovation potential, competitiveness and

---

[2] http://www.balticsupply.eu/

productivity and to stimulate international cooperation in order to improve access to the European market.

4. Measures and SME involvement

Initially BalticSupply analysed the regional economies and their procurement policies and compiled industry data bases for each supply cluster. Additionally, a database of existing cluster organisations and their services for SMEs were set up and made available for all project partners.

After that the project partners developed a comprehensive service portfolio for SME promotion on interregional supply markets. These online and offline services were integrated in the "European Business Support Network"[3]. SMEs can register with the platform and can gain access to foreign markets, find information about tendering procedures and trainings and get in contact with potential business partners.

The partners of the European Business Support Network engaged in a number of offline activities, e.g. organised conferences, workshops and business matchmaking events for SMEs.

The European Business Support Network continues to operate after the end of BalticSupply in December 2012. The network is still growing and open to new members.

5. Examples and best results

In October 2012 the BalticSupply-partner Klaipeda Science and Technology Park (KSTP) organised the East Link Conference in Klaipeda, Lithuania. Part of the conference was a BalticSupply workshop on a geothermal fish farm project planned in Lithuania. The workshop was attended by BalticSupply partners from Latvia, Germany and Denmark as well as a large number of experts and actors in the fish farm industry.

---

[3] http://www.eubizz.net

KSTP led the formation of a interregional tendering partnership of SME fish farm suppliers which combine a wide range of knowledge, contacts and experience in marine food production, fish farm biology, aquaculture technology, energy and project management. During the workshop the participants agreed to complete the project design. The next steps will focus on the last stages of the supply chain. These include technology suppliers, financing experts and investors, as well as business managers for practical fish farm operations.

2 I Baltic Fashion[4]

1. Project in a nutshell

Innovation is the key to success. This holds especially true for a struggling economic sectors like the fashion industry in the Baltic Sea Region. The Baltic Fashion project developed innovative approaches for supporting fashions SMEs and explored possibilities of transnational cooperation.

2. Project partners

The Baltic Fashion project comprised 11 partners representing fashion design schools, fashion associations, business incubators active in the field as well as regional development authorities. The Municipality of Heringsdorf (Mecklenburg-Vorpommern, Germany) acted as Lead Partner.

3. Aims of the project

The aim of the project was to create a suitable support infrastructure for an innovative fashion industry at national level as well as across the Baltic Sea region. Baltic Fashion did not only make a positive contribution to the economic development of the region, but also to its overall sustainability. It promoted eco-friendly production and materials as well as regional production, contributed to women entrepreneurship and strengthened cultural identity.

4. Measures and SME involvement

Despite the fact that the production of clothes has been shifting to Asia in the last decades, the fashion sector is still of importance to BSR economies. The Baltic fashion sector is mainly composed of SMEs, with a large share of females not only in services and administration but also in production (80% in new member states). Still fashion companies, especially start-ups, struggle to sell their products.

---

[4] http://www.balticfashion.eu/

In the course of the Baltic Fashion project the main challenges were analysed and possible remedies presented. Best practices of support programmes and business-training programmes were developed and tested. Fashion innovations with regard to sustainability, niche markets and materials/technologies were analysed and disseminated to SMEs as well as support structures in the BSR. Furthermore, the first ever-comprehensive BSR fashion web-platform (www.balticfashion.eu), which contains easily accessible, integrated and centralised information on the fashion sector and related support and training opportunities, was set up. This platform creates the basis for increased transnational cooperation in the fashion sector.

5. Examples and best results

With regard to innovation analyses the concepts "From Trash to Trend" and "Fashion Empowerment" are particularly successful. "From Trash to Trend" aims to share design globally while finding and using left-over textile materials locally. This is achieved through an internet platform that connects manufacturers with leftover textiles and designers in need of textiles. Through "Fashion empowerment" collections are developed for groups marginalized by the mainstream fashion industry, e.g. nursing mothers, people in wheelchairs or blind people.

A very successful fashion support programme is "Coppice". "Coppice" is a quality label from the Art Academy of Latvia which is granted to recent graduates to market their products.

An innovative concept in the category of business training is the "B2B speed dating". Experts from different fields share their knowledge with fashion designers in 15 minutes sessions. Apart from that, each participant meets another participant in a blind date, which offers additional possibilities for networking.

These and other innovative concepts developed by the Baltic Fashion partners can be found on the Baltic Fashion web-portal and are presented in a concise, summarised way in the "Baltic Fashion findings" report as well as "Baltic Fashion Innovation Digest" (available as downloads from the web portal).

3 I BaSIC[5]

1. Project in a nutshell

The objective of BaSIC was to create a seamless working environment for fast growth innovative small and medium enterprises (SME) all over the Baltic Sea Region, embedded in a reliable network of leading science parks and clusters. Emphasis had been given to identify, select, train and coach promising SMEs, and to provide them with harmonised access to markets and funding for internationalisation and growth.

2. Project partners

BaSIC (Baltic Sea Innovation Network Centres) was led by WISTA-MANAGEMENT, a management company owned by the City of Berlin to develop and operate the science park "Adlershof". The project consortium consists of science parks, incubators and innovation facilitators as well as public authorities.

3. Aims of the project

The Baltic Sea markets are full of obstacles hindering growth of SMEs. The regional markets are still disconnected, so that innovative, expanding SMEs are suffering from different regulations, legislations, financing conditions, rules for investing, etc. Science parks and business incubators offer services for growth and funding only on a regional level – these services are not networked, harmonised and transferable.

This was where BaSIC walked on stage: It developed transferable tools and instruments for a quick, improved, harmonised market access.

---

[5] http://www.basic-net.eu/

4. Measures and SME involvement

a) Market information

BaSIC developed and distributed market information instruments regarding legal aspects, tax regulations, company forms, etc. for companies that are planning to settle in or expand to other parts of the Baltic Sea Region by

- developing a market access guide,

- organising training events for companies on how to establish a business in the BSR.

b) Technology information

BaSIC provided technology information by developing cluster reports presenting the potential of BSR markets in Photonics, Micro and Nano Technologies; Information and Communication Technologies; Life Sciences.

c) Brokering and cluster events

Three B2B meetings and three cluster events for the above mentioned business sectors were organised for companies to find cooperation partners.

During the three-year-period of BaSIC more than 200 innovative, fast growing companies have been supported by the project partners and put in touch with potential business partners.

5. Examples and best results

Market Access Points

The project partners established so called Market Access Point (MAP) in each of the biggest metropolitan areas of the Baltic Sea Region: Berlin, Copenhagen, Helsinki, Oslo, Riga, Stockholm, Tallinn, Vilnius, Warsaw and St. Petersburg.

The Market Access Points are run by a Local Case Manager who guides enterprises and entrepreneurs into the region (and also regional enterprises that want to expand outwards to other parts of the BSR). Supported by a network of experts, the MAP Case Manager assists in entering the market. The service provides advice and practical support in the process of establishing a legal entity and starting a business in the region.

After having settled in the new market, the enterprises receive operational support regarding business development, planning, recruitment and investment services, finance and funds.

4 I BONITA[6]

1. Project in a nutshell

BONITA was focused on the transfer of innovative technologies from public research organisations to SMEs, which does not work effectively in the Baltic Sea Region. The project did not pursue a practical approach but rather took a step back and analysed the general structures, processes and mechanisms of technology transfer. Based on this research BONITA developed an enhanced transfer model that can be used as a checklist by innovation transfer organisations of any kind to improve their results.

2. Project partners

BONITA (Baltic Organisation and Network of Innovation Transfer Associations) was led by the University of Bremen, coordinating 14 project partners from seven countries, ranging from universities and public authorities to research and technological development supporters.

3. Aims of the project

Research cooperation as well as knowledge transfer between public research organisations and industry are insufficiently developed within the European innovation system. Although universities are important developers of new technologies and products, their technological and service based innovations often are not transferred to the private sector for commercialisation.

This deficit has two main reasons: 1) The necessary organisational structures guiding innovation transfer are weak, and 2) SMEs often have little resources in terms of budget, time and manpower to invest in new technologies and to adapt these to their

---

[6] www.bonita-project.eu

19

specific needs. BONITA focussed on the facilitating structures and processes that support or sometimes hinder the successful transfer of technology innovations from research organisations to companies.

4. Measures

Within the BONITA project existing technology and innovation transfer models throughout the Baltic Sea Region were evaluated in order to derive an enhanced transfer model as an adequate innovation facilitating structure.

The project partners extracted the success factors from surveyed innovation transfer organisations and developed a model called innoSPICE. innoSPICE allows analysing the structures and quality of technology transfer processes in a given organisation. This assessment provides the fundament to improve the effectiveness of organisations that are dedicated to transfer innovations, knowledge and technology.

As a next step innoSPICE could help to develop certificates that research organisations or innovation transfer organisations could obtain. These certificates could be very useful to acquire external funding or find (business) partners for research cooperation.

Furthermore BONITA established the BSR-wide BONITA Transnational Network consisting of the project partners. The network continues to operate after the project ended in 2012 and the network partners are responsible for training and consultation on BONITA's technology transfer model. The network partners also support the generation and transfer of innovations regarding the regions' leading technologies (e.g. wearable computing, e-learning, robotics).

As an element to present and promote the research and development capacities of the participating research institutions, BONITA implemented seven exemplary physical showrooms. These showrooms enable marketing of research results towards local industry and facilitate new possibilities of collaboration between academia, industry and public offices. The showrooms offer meeting spaces equipped with conferencing equipment as well as the latest multimedia technologies that allow web enabled interactive prototype demonstrations.

5 I BSHR HealthPort[7]

1. The project in a nutshell

BSHR HealthPort addresses key bottlenecks in health care innovations like insufficient commercial exploitation of solutions proposed by health care researchers and practitioners; procurement practices limiting SME access to the health care market; insufficient innovation competencies of target groups. BSHR HealthPort bridges gaps between health care providers and SMEs. The ideas from clinics are transferred into business environment through idea competition and direct business support measures. BSHR HealthPort provides involved actors with the necessary business skills; supports SME in procurement practices and promotes SME access to financing. BSHR HealthPort launched an innovation agenda „Driving cross-sectoral innovation in health and life sciences - An Innovation Agenda for the Baltic Sea Region Health Economy".

2. Project partners

BSHR HealthPort was led by ScanBalt® fmba, a not-for-profit membership association of public and private health and life science clusters and organisations. Other partners were University of Gothenburg, Sweden, North Denmark Region, Denmark, Culminatum Innovation Ltd, Finland, Entrepreneurship Development Centre for Biotechnology and Medicine, Estonia, BioCon Valley, Germany, Turku Science Park Ltd, Finland, InnoBaltica, Poland, Institute of Biotechnology, Vilnius University, Lithuania. The project cooperated with 14 associated partners (organisations of healthcare providers, SMEs and decision makers).

3. Aims of the project

BSHR HealthPort focus on the interactions between Health Service providers and SMEs with the aim of enhancing innovation, reduce health care costs and promote

---

[7] http://www.scanbalt.org/projects/scanbalt+health+region

SME access to the BSR Health Care market. Health care is not only a cost for society but also as a driver of a competitive and knowledge based health economy. BSHR HealthPort promotes a strong and sustainable Baltic Sea Region health economy. BSHR HealthPort is a project within the flagship ScanBalt Health Region of the EU Strategy for the Baltic Sea Region's Action Plan. The ultimate goals of ScanBalt Health Region are to assist promoting a knowledge based globally competitive health economy in the Baltic Sea Region; to assist solving the grand societal challenges of health within the region and to play a strong role on global health.

4. Measures and SME involvement

a) Facilitation of SMEs' market access. SMEs were invited to matchmakings with regional key actors and joined R&D projects.

b) Promotion of SME business development. BSHR HealthPort offered support in procurement practises and supported SMEs' access to financing.

c) Enhancement of innovation competencies among healthcare providers and SME managers.

d) Implementation of an idea competition for healthcare practitioners to create new SMEs or enable growth of existing SMEs.

e) Promoting the development of Accelerate Life, a ecross-border acceleration platform for health-tech start-up companies with shared methodology, networks, expertise and resources.

d) Promoting the development of the Nordic-Baltic Accelerace Investment Fund (NBAIF). NBAIF will be an early stage fund, investing in companies that have been through the AL Programme.

e) Preparation of an innovation agenda aiming to improve healthcare, reduce healthcare costs and enhance regional economic development by promoting a BSR innovation eco-system for health care.

5. Examples and best results

a) Concept of an annual idea competition in health care in the Baltic Sea Region

BSHR HealthPort organised competitions for healthcare innovations. The awards were granted to innovations like medical and therapeutic tools and technologies, diagnostics, laboratory and hospital furniture and technology, and services. The innovations should lead to commercialized products or services. The winners of the innovation competitions received tailor-made expert coaching for the business development of their innovations: After basic coaching, the best cases among the winners were selected for advanced coaching including the possibility to start negotiations with suitable financing bodies.

b) Pilot cases for commercialisation

Two business cases were chosen for tailor-made support by the project partners in order to reach swift commercialisation.

c) Interviews

To understand risks and barriers at stake in the ScanBalt Health Region interviews with SMEs, clusters organizations; science parks and hospitals were conducted in the consortium regions as there is an increasing demand for healthcare services and solutions that have the potential to reduce health care costs, improve resource allocation in hospitals and provide improved care to the patients.

d) Entrepreneurial education

Having the knowledge about procurement rules and processes, staying competitive in the procurement process will make a huge difference. Based on a report a number of courses were developed and vetted.

e) Educational platform

Training to bring up the competence of the management was brought out to be a key factor for success for SMEs. Therefore a concept for a web-based educational tool for ScanBalt Health Region was developed. The e-learning platform should be combined with regional mentoring to boost regional economic development.

f) Promoting infrastructures supporting healthtech start-ups and financing

HealthPort promoted the establishment of the before mentioned **Accelerate Life and** the Nordic-Baltic Accelerace Investment Fund.

g) Preparation of an innovation agenda

The innovation agenda "Driving cross-sectoral innovation in health and life sciences - An Innovation Agenda for the Baltic Sea Region Health Economy" has been discussed throughout the BSR and with the EU and other relevant stakeholders. The agenda is very well received and implementation has already begun with development of concepts and set-up of concrete innovation platforms within selected thematic areas.

h) Promoting BSR to investors, companies and talents

The HealthPort press study tour to Denmark 28th to 30th of May 2013 was fully booked with 12 participating journalists, the maximum number the tour could host, and with many more on the waiting list. The tour focused on commercialisation of ideas from clinics and hospitals, gave an insight into the Danish health and life science sectors as a practical example and discussed the future of health and bio economy. As a result e.g. an article in the prestigious Scientific American was published entitled "Innovation and collaboration are keys to success in the Baltic Sea Region".

6 I BSR InnoReg[8]

1. Project in a nutshell

The project focused on increasing the effectiveness of regional innovation support activities by improving the strategic know-how of business development organisations (BDOs) operating outside metropolitan areas. The project helped business development organisations to improve business development and innovation support services for small and medium-sized enterprises.

The project partners also brought local and regional decision makers together to discuss global economic challenges and to agree on an innovation policy memorandum.

2. Project partners

BSR InnoReg (Strengthening Innovation Governance in Baltic Non-metropolitan Regions through Transnational Cooperation) was led by the Baltic Institute of Finland (Suomen Itämeri-instituutti), a not-for-profit organisation dedicated to promote cooperation in the Baltic Sea Region. The project consisted of 18 partners from six Baltic Sea Region countries. The partners represented local, regional and national authorities as well as science parks and technology centres.

3. Aims of the project

Innovation is most of the times associated with large cities, and a large share of attention and funds for innovation promotion is directed to metropolitan areas. But the less densely populated areas of the Baltic Sea Region and their enterprises have got their own potential for being innovative, and for the regional development they play a pivotal role. Therefore BSR InnoReg focussed its measures mainly on the existing business development organisations in these areas.

4. Measures and best results

---

[8] http://www.baltic.org/bsrinnoreg

a) Baltic Innovation Policy Memorandum

The partner regions of the BSR InnoReg project have agreed on key issues for the development of innovation activities in the nonmetropolitan areas of the Baltic Sea Region. Among these are:

- Developing an innovation policy framework that takes into account the needs of the nonmetropolitan regions.

- Strengthening the regional dimension of innovation policy to cater for the regions' specific assets and opportunities.

- Targeting innovation in the traditionally strong sectors. Innovation support often targets high-tech sectors and products. But there is potential for innovation and growth as well in the traditional sectors like manufacturing and services that are often to be found being predominant in non-metropolitan areas.

- Better support for new modes of innovation in the nonmetropolitan regions. Open innovation, user and demand driven innovation, organisational innovation and social innovation are becoming more important; regional innovation policy measures need to take that into account.

b) Innovation support tools and practices

Various innovation support measures were developed and tested by partners. The results were compiled in a handbook, summarising all piloted activities, as well as gathered experience and recommendations. Some examples are:

- **Innovation vouchers**. Voucher systems offer small grants to encourage first and small innovation activities of SMEs. These grants can be used for consulting by research institutions or small R&D projects. In the German federal state Brandenburg for example, two voucher types of up to 1500 Euros and up to 7000 Euro are offered by Brandenburg's public bank for business promotion. In the first 11 months more than 120 SMEs applied for vouchers. One important lesson learnt was: Mediators or knowledge brokers, e.g. technology and innovation transfer offices at universities, are crucial for bridging the gap between SMEs and research institutions. The voucher system proved to be a flexible and unbureaucratic tool. There is evidence that regional voucher systems lead to more innovation activities in SMEs, especially in small and micro-enterprises.

- **Living Labs**. A Living Lab is a tool for real live tests of innovations integrating ordinary users. The users do the testing while working, living or playing in a real-life environment. Yet there are only a few Living Labs operating in Europe, one of them is the Agro Living Lab (ALL) in Seinäjoki, a town in the West of Finland. ALL is run by the regional development company Frami, the Seinäjoki University of Applied Sciences and the Ruralia Institute at the University of Helsinki. ALL is focused on the usability and user-centred design of technologies in agriculture and forestry. Within the InnoReg project Frami tested ALL in an international context in order to find out to what extent user needs and product requirements depend on the particular country and culture. This knowledge is precious for SMEs aiming to enter new international markets. Frami carried out pilot case studies in Estonia and Poland, working with local farmers in the Agro Living Lab. The results obtained from these case studies confirm that user needs and product requirements depend to a considerable degree on the country and the culture. This experience is now being used to further develop the Agro Living Lab.

7 I BSR QUICK[9]

1. Project in a nutshell

BSR QUICK connected the academic world with SMEs by establishing the Baltic Sea Academy. This unique network of 15 universities and polytechnics delivers tangible R&D solutions and innovation transfers to SMEs, and it offers trainings and study curricula specified to the needs of SME entrepreneurs and skilled employees in the region. The Baltic Sea Academy is cooperating very closely with the Hanse-Parlament, a non-profit network of business chambers, building a powerful innovation platform of SME organisations and universities for the benefit of the companies in the region.

2. Project partners

BSR QUICK (Qualification, Innovation, Cooperation and Key business for Small and Medium Enterprises in the Baltic Sea Region) was led by the Hanse-Parlament, coordinating 40 formal partners and 42 associated partners ranging from chambers to universities and public authorities.

3. Aims of the project

The most significant barriers for SME growth in the Baltic Sea Region are a) the shortage of qualified entrepreneurs, managers and skilled employees, and b) the lack of adequate innovation support for SMEs.

BSR QUICK offers a structured and coordinated approach to increase the innovation potential of SMEs and the knowledge and skills of entrepreneurs and employees. Universities and SME promoters like chambers cooperate in three clusters (Human resources and organisational development; Energy, climate and environmental protection; Construction technologies) generating R&D solutions and facilitating their

---

[9] http://www.bsr-quick.eu/

implementation in SMEs, as well as developing and upgrading vocational and academic training programmes.

4. Measures and SME involvement

After having identified three areas of outstanding SME innovation deficits (Human resources and organisational development; Energy, climate and environmental protection; Construction technologies), BSR QUICK established the Baltic Sea Academy (BSA[10]) which continues to operate after the end of the project in 2012. The BSA is a network of 15 universities in nine countries that are dedicated to support innovation and R&D in SMEs of the above mentioned clusters. Each university is specialised to promote innovations regarding a certain topic in the whole Baltic Sea Region. In close cooperation with 47 chambers the outreach of the BSA covers the entire Baltic Sea Region. The BSA's innovation promotion is realised through personal counselling and business forums as well as newsletters, internet platforms and electronic tools. Already during the project universities and chambers have developed concrete investment plans and realised R&D solutions for more than 686 SMEs in the region.

Within the second important pillar of BSR QUICK – education – curricula for four new training courses were developed and realised with 952 participants and transferred BSR-wide. In accordance with urgent SMEs needs six existing technology training courses were selected and also transferred BSR-wide. With the support of BSR QUICK three dual-degree programmes were promoted and implemented by two universities.

5. Examples and best results

Dual Degree Programmes

Among several educational measures, dual bachelor study courses were developed, e.g. the Dual Bachelor Study Course "Renewable Energies". These dual study courses

---

[10] http://www.baltic-sea-academy.eu

meet the needs of SMEs much better than regular university study courses that are too theoretical. During dual study courses students get credit points for their academic work at the university and at the same time for their practical training in a company. The students graduate as "bachelors" (which allows to pursue an academic career in master or PhD programmes) and at the same time receive a skilled worker degree. SMEs are highly appreciative for these students that already have practical training; therefore students usually have excellent job offers before graduation. Also these students play a vital role in bridging the gap between SMEs and academia, allowing a constant exchange even many years after graduation.

Investment and business plans

As part of the BSR QUICK project more than 600 individual business and investment plans were realised to support SMEs in 10 countries. After companies had approached chambers or universities, the plans were discussed and jointly developed, securing that the plans really fits the specific needs of the company.

In Gdansk this was so successful that a consultant for these plans stayed permanently employed at the chamber after the project ended. Companies that used to have difficulties getting a loan or start-up credit from banks succeeded after having reviewed their business plans by the chamber. At the same time, the banks appreciated that a rather independent or public organisation like a university or chamber supported the SMEs instead of private consultants.

8 I IBI NET[11]

1. Project in a nutshell

IBI NET was enhancing the cooperation of business incubators in the Baltic Sea Region. Seven business incubators and technology centres in six BSR countries now cooperate and communicate on a regular basis using a unique Internet platform. The network helps business incubators to offer business support services based on best practice in the region.

2. Project partners

IBI NET (Intercountry Business Incubators' Network) was led by Riga Planning Region (RPR), the planning authority for Riga and the surrounding region. RPR co-ordinated the cooperation of six other partners representing regional and local authorities, universities, business incubators and technology centres from Norway, Sweden, Latvia, Belarus, Poland, and Germany. The Leningrad Business Support Centre was associated partner.

3. Aims of the project

Business incubators are important agents in nurturing and promoting the development of innovative and export oriented SMEs. Every region around the Baltic Sea has got its own business incubators, with multiple instruments and procedures to support start-ups and young, growing enterprises. The diversity of incubator organisations is a rich source for project members to learn from each other. Therefore IBI NET aimed to establish a transnational business incubator network as a platform to continuously exchange information, know-how, experience and technologies in order to foster the development of innovative SMEs in the entire Baltic Sea Region. The international network helps business incubators to offer support services based on best practice gathered in the region. Equally, it inspires policy makers on national and

[11] http://www.ibi-net.eu/

regional levels to build innovation and business support systems based on examples of leaders in innovation systems in the region.

4. Measures and best results

The starting point was the analysis of the capacity and practices of business incubators in the partner countries, specifically looking at financing, services offered and the direction of future development and needs of the organisation.

The next step was the creation of IBI Net – a network of business incubators from Latvia, Sweden, Norway, Germany, Poland and Belarus. It was and still is used for experience exchange activities and benchmarking for business incubation services. Part of IBI Net is the Internet portal www.ibi-net.eu that can be used by the IBI Net members and their companies. The online portal contains information about the business incubators' products, services, cooperation offers, business proposals and contact information. It provides an automatic and manual tool to collect information from business incubator websites and a search tool. In the lifetime of the project, IBI Net was formalized into the Association of business incubators having its operational work plan – IBI Net Guidelines – that is being realized beyond the project.

Together the project partners developed an ICT tool to monitor and steer the performance of enterprises supported by incubators (developing company growth plans, setting milestones, coordinating coaching within business plans, recording, monitoring and evaluating the company's progress).

Furthermore IBI Net issued financial guidelines outlining funding options for business incubators based on the best practice in the region.

9 I JOSEFIN[12]

1. Project in a nutshell

The JOSEFIN project identified the lack of access to suitable finance as a main barrier to internationalisation for innovative SMEs from the Baltic Sea Region. The goal of the project was to promote innovation and internationalisation in SMEs by facilitating better access to finance.

The partners of the JOSEFIN project developed and implemented advanced financial support instruments of two categories – individual coaching of SMEs and the provision of financial support.

2. Project partners

The project Joint SME Finance for Innovation (JOSEFIN) was led by the Investitionsbank Berlin. The partnership in JOSEFIN consisted of 23 public financial institutions, SME support organisations and regional authorities from seven BSR countries.

3. Aims of the project

Regional development in the 21st century depends in parts on the ability of a region's enterprises to compete successfully on international markets. Most SMEs however are rooted in local and regional markets and are having difficulties to enter foreign markets to grow and develop their business. The main reasons for this are lack of strategic thinking within the management of many SMEs and the reluctance of banks to provide SMEs with funding for innovation and internationalisation projects.

JOSEFIN aimed to provide SMEs with individual coaching that would help them to develop their innovation and internationalisation strategy, and raise their attractiveness and ability to get access to finance. On the other hand JOSEFIN developed a

---

[12] http://www.josefin-org.eu

new financial instrument that allows reducing the risk for banks that are willing to fund innovative SMEs.

4. Measures and SME involvement

The main result of the project is the so called JOSEFIN Service Model which consists of a loan guarantee instrument and coaching services.

a) JOSEFIN Loan Guarantee Model

The main element is a risk-sharing construction that distributes the risk that an SME may fail to repay a loan over different institutions. The loan issuing institution has got the possibility to involve other financing institutions in the securitisation of the loan (JOSEFIN Loan Guarantee Model). The risk sharing partner can be a public guarantee fund, a guarantee bank, or another public or semi-public provider of loan guarantees.

The distribution of potential so called credit defaults reduces the risk for the bank issuing the loan to the SME. This process makes it more likely for SMEs to get loans.

b) JOSEFIN Service Model

To support companies in the process of preparing and implementing investment projects for innovation as well as internationalisation, additional non-financial services are offered. These coaching services cover three phases of support: information, project development and project implementation. Due to the coaches' support the chances will raise that the project becomes a success – as this also reduces the risk of credit defaults, the non-financial services raise the chances of SMEs to get a loan from a bank.

5. Examples and best results

Until the end of the project in January 2012 the JOSEFIN Loan Guarantee helped to generate loans to SMEs of 153.9 million Euro in total.

Case Study 1: Loan guarantee for Pumacy Technologies

Pumacy Technologies is a provider of knowledge, innovation, and process management solutions with a holistic approach ranging from a first strategy and systematic analysis to a professional concept and the implementation of the final solution. Pumacy Technologies intended to provide a central point of contact for client queries regarding product lifecycle management (PLM). For this, the office Berlin was to be extended to include the "Innovation Centre PLM" where companies from traditional manufacturing sectors as well as growth sectors like life sciences or new energies can learn to streamline their product development processes by using innovative software technologies.

The challenge for Pumacy Technologies was to manage investments amounting within a short period of 18 months to a multiple level of what would be conventional in this period of time. For this, Pumacy had to provide additional securities. The loan guarantee scheme "Berlin Kredit Innovativ" that the Investitionsbank Berlin (IBB) had developed within the JOSEFIN project was the key to success. The IBB offered Pumacy's house bank a 60% guarantee, and in cooperation with the IBB, Pumacy was able to organise the overall financing plan within a few weeks and convinced the house bank of the benefits of the project – and a loan of €500.000 was issued to Pumacy.

Case Study 2: Coaching Service for Superior Metals Sweden

Superior Metals Sweden has developed a casted alloy and a method to control the properties of it. The business idea is based on research performed at the KTH Royal Institute of Technology in Stockholm. Two different applications had been identified and the company was working with two costumers to develop a product.

The investment project aimed to support the working capital of the company, to test the properties of the developed products as well as to research the market. The company had a shortage of funding and the development of the alloy towards a sellable product was very time consuming. Superior Metals have received support through the JOSEFIN service model by business coaching of 12 hours per month during 2011. After the company had received financial guidance from a coach and an incubator, it applied for financing. The financial support has so far consisted of grants, but loans are likely in the near future.

.

10 I   PlasTEP[13]

1. Project in a nutshell

PlasTEP aimed at raising awareness among decision makers in industry and politics of the possibilities that low-temperature plasma technologies are offering to protect the environment. By disseminating information and initiating contacts to politicians and potential customers, PlasTEP stimulated innovation transfer from research institutions to industry users and the implementation of plasma technologies in industrial processes.

2. Project partners

PlasTEP (Dissemination and fostering of plasma based technological innovation for environment protection in BSR) was led by the Technologiezentrum Fördergesellschaft Vorpommern (TZV), an independent service provider and incubator for companies in Western Pomerania. TZV coordinated 14 further partners from eight countries, consisting of universities, research institutions and associations of engineers.

3. Aims of the project

Low-temperature plasma technologies have made a lot of progress in recent years, innovative solutions allow cleaning polluted water or exhaust gases. But these smart technologies are rarely implemented in industrial processes yet. Only in a few places plasma technologies developed by research institutes in the BSR have been applied in practice for environmental protection.

Therefore the main objective of PlasTEP was to present applied plasma based cleaning technologies to the general public and to stakeholders in politics and industry in order to establish a market driven transfer process and an increasing number of applications.

---

[13] http://www.plastep.eu/

The project partners were involved in four working groups with different thematic priorities. One group worked on fostering plasma-based methods to reduce nitrogen and sulphur oxides (NOx/SOx), primarily occurring during all burning processes. The second group concentrated on volatile organic compounds (VOCs) and particles that appear during e.g. polymer processing.

A smaller group dealt with cleaning polluted surface water. This technology-oriented work groups were supplemented by an umbrella group responsible for environmental aspects and educational activities.

4. Measures and SME involvement

To attract investors, several field tests were successfully performed, e.g. to reduce odour at a water plant in Poland and at a chicken farm in Germany, and to reduce VOC in the chemical industry in Estonia. For this purpose, the PlasTEP partners had developed mobile plasma devices and analytics which can be installed at test sites for technical studies.

The results of these real condition field tests were presented to SMEs at PlasTEP workshops in eight countries. These workshops proved to be the most effective way to get in contact with stakeholders from industry and politics and to initiate technology transfer.

In preparation of the workshops and field tests, providers of services to SMEs were contacted. They were informed about the possibilities and new trends in plasma technologies and access to new technologies (e.g. by licenses from the institutes). Another way information about plasma technologies was distributed was the handbook "Plasma Treatment for Environment Protection", that the project partners had produced.

During the PlasTEP project three summer schools were organised. The second and the third summer school were combined with a training course for participants from the industry. The combination of both types of audiences – students and industry professionals – was very fruitful.

During the two week event an intensive exchange of knowledge not only from the lectures to the participants took place. Furthermore the students got to know the practical perspective of the industry participants, who in turn learnt to understand the scientific interest in plasma technologies. These events opened the way for international long term cooperation. Some interested participants of the summer school are still in contact to exchange their knowledge.

Within PlasTEP some partners applied for an extension stage project PlasTEP+ to continue the practical demonstration of the potential of plasma technologies.

All materials and presentations are addressed particularly to engineers and stakeholders from the industry and will be further distributed by PlasTEP+ activities. First discussions about new investments in plasma based air cleaning technologies started within the project.

11 I   QUICK IGA[14]

1. Project in a nutshell

QUICK IGA identified the lack of skilled personnel as one of the main hindrances for innovation growth. And given the fact that a high diversity of work force positively influences the innovation climate in a company, QUICK IGA was supporting the reintegration of elderly employees in companies and promoting a higher rate of female employees and female entrepreneurship. The project transferred knowledge and best practice mainly from Scandinavia to the southern parts of the BSR, because the northern countries achieved gender equality and the integration of elderly in the labour market to a far greater extent than all other BSR countries.

2. Project partners

QUICK IGA (Innovative SMEs by Gender and Age) was led by the Hanse-Parlament, coordinating twelve partners ranging from chambers to universities, research institutes and education facilitators from eight BSR countries.

3. Aims of the project

The population in the Baltic Sea Region is aging; the number of people of working age will be decreasing by up to 20% until the year 2030. This adds a lot of pressure on SMEs which already nowadays are struggling to find skilled personnel. This lack of skilled workforce is limiting growth and innovations in SMEs today and will do so even more in the future.

At the same time a lot of women and older people – who represent a significant part of the qualified workforce – are not fully employed in many countries, particularly in the southern parts of the Baltic Sea Region. The employment rate of women ranges from 53% in Poland to 74% in Norway, the rate of older people from 32% in Poland to 70% in Sweden.

---

[14] http://quick-iga.eu/

The QUICK IGA project addressed both of these problems simultaneously. It supported the development and adjustment of working and organisational structures in SMEs in order to increase the employment rate of women and elderly people, as their integration in the labour market mitigates the scarcity of skilled workforce and at the same time increases the innovation capacity of SMEs.

4. Measures

QUICK IGA started with economic and structure analyses and forecasts for the BSR countries as well as analyses of the education and labour markets in the BSR. The results were published in a book and presented at international conferences. The analyses clearly revealed the need to integrate more women and reintegrate more elderly people in the BSR labour markets.

Therefore QUICK IGA developed a concept promoting the ability to work (aimed at elderly people) and for gender management (aimed at equal chances for women).

In parallel the QUICK IGA partners collected and analysed cases of best practice in promoting the employment of women and older people in the Baltic Sea Region, focussing mainly on Scandinavia. The first three best practices were transferred to all project partners and 65 transfer partners.

In order to spread information and concepts how to integrate women and elderly in SMEs and how to stimulate entrepreneurship among women, adequate qualification of trainers within disseminating organisations like chambers is needed. These trainers are then supposed to instruct consultants who work with SMEs and entrepreneurs directly. The curriculum for a train the trainer programme was developed and a seminar with the participation of lecturers from Baltic countries was carried out. Also the curriculum for training of consultants was developed, followed by two trainings in Belarus and Poland.

Three memorandums of common understanding for Latvia, Lithuania and Poland were developed and signed by different stakeholders. The three memorandums were of a surprisingly strong interest in politics, administration and interest groups in Latvia, Lithuania and Poland, who participated at national conferences in these countries.

5. Examples and best results

Memorandum of understanding

Three memorandums of understanding were signed during national conferences in Latvia, Lithuania and Poland. The objective was to secure the sustainability, raise awareness of female employees and the re-integration of elderly into companies, and to win new stakeholders.

Content of the signed memorandum:

- increasing the proportion of women in leadership positions in SMEs,

- support of start-ups by women, strengthening the long-term viability of new businesses and increase of the number of women-entrepreneurs,

- medium and long-term increase of labour force participation of women and older people in general,

- sustainable improvement of vocational training as well as the strengthening of personal competence,

- strengthening of innovation and productivity in SMEs, improving the income situation and achieving "equal pay for equal work".

At the conference in Vilnius three ministries signed the memorandum of understanding, agreeing to actively promote female and older employees in their country on a long lasting basis. Even though it seems just another paper signed, the impact is quite evident. In Latvia the memorandum will result for example in up to twelve local conferences in different regions in the next years to boost female entrepreneurship.

12 I ScienceLink[15]

1. Project in a nutshell

SCIENCE LINK established an international cooperation network of the four large-scale research infrastructures in the Baltic Sea Region with universities and innovation promoters. The research infrastructures – DESY in Hamburg, the Max IV Laboratory in Lund, the Helmholtz-Zentrum Berlin and the Helmholtz-Zentrum Geesthacht – are using photon and neutron sources for scientific research but are also offering R&D cooperation to enterprises. SCIENCE LINK aimed to increase the commercial use of the four large-scale research infrastructures in order to promote product and service innovations in the Baltic Sea Region.

2. Project partners

SCIENCE LINK was led by DESY Deutsches Elektronen Synchrotron, a national research centre located in Hamburg operating particle accelerators. DESY coordinated 18 project partners ranging from research facilities to universities and public innovation and development agencies.

3. Aims of the project

There is a cluster of large-scale photon and neutron research infrastructure in the Baltic Sea Region and more large-scale research centres are planned (the European XFEL in Hamburg, ESS in Lund, Solaris in Krakow). These expensive infrastructures must not be disconnected islands. Structures for cooperation need to be established and especially, companies from the entire Baltic Sea Region should get access to the research infrastructures for R&D projects.

But yet there is only little information accessible for companies about the resources and services available at the research infrastructures and how they could be used commercially. Additionally, supporting structures and services are needed as SMEs

---

[15] http://www.science-link.eu/

do not have their own research departments or measurement experts. When they have a problem, someone familiar with the research infrastructures has to translate it into scientific terms and prepare measurements for finding solutions. Through such access to large-scale research infrastructure companies can develop better products and become more competitive.

4. Measures and SME involvement

At the beginning of the project the network and the website www.science-link.eu was established.

The universities and innovation and development agencies play a crucial role within the SCIENCE LINK network. The regional innovation/development agencies advertise the R&D cooperation offers of the four large-scale research infrastructures (RIs), have established contact points and are actively contacting companies.

The universities consult, accompany and support the companies before, during and after the measurements at the RIs. For this reason there are Industrial Liaison Officers employed at the RIs and at the other scientific partner institutions in order to help and inform companies in their national languages.

After Science Link was established a first call for companies was published. The companies were offered free measurement time in the large-scale research infrastructures. There were ten applications by companies of which eight were approved. The Industrial Liaison officers (ILOs) at the RIs and the other partners started their work supporting the companies and preparing the measurements.

The ILOs were employed at an early stage and trained in all participating RIs in order to be able to support the companies and to link the companies and the measurement experts at the RIs.

In the frame of the 2nd call, published in the autumn 2012, 21 companies applied for beam time and 19 applications were accepted. The applications came from a broad variety of branches, and 70% of the companies were SMEs.

Four companies from the first call and five from the second call have already carried out their measurements.

13 I   StarDust[16]

1. Project in a nutshell

The objective of StarDust was to find new answers to big challenges that Baltic Sea Region is facing: increasing water pollution, ageing population, future transport solutions and new digital business. StarDust turned these challenges into opportunities for economic growth. Researchers, clusters, SME networks and public actors from different countries around the Baltic Sea jointly addressed these challenges in four sub-projects, fostering innovations of all kinds (scientific, technical as well as non-technical) with the aim to develop commercial products and services.

2. Project partners

StarDust (The Strategic Project on Trans-national Commercial Activities in Research & Innovation, Clusters and in SME-Networks) is led by VINNOVA, Sweden's government agency for innovation. In total, StarDust consisted of 34 partners from the public and semi-public sector. These partners were supported by 33 associated partners from national, regional and local levels. This set of partners represented all national ministries and innovation agencies in the ten Baltic Sea countries. During 2012 and 2013 StarDust has strengthened its partnership by attracting new partners and financiers: the partners received more than 8 MEUR as add-on investment, 15 research institutions and six new cluster and business development organisations joined as associated partners.

3. Aims of the project

StarDust aimed to create transnational innovation platforms for each of the four big future challenges for the Baltic Sea Region (water pollution, ageing population, transport solutions, new digital business). These cooperation platforms were to be supported by new tools and methods on open and user-driven innovation.

---

[16] http://www.bsrstars.se/stardust/

Each of the four projects combined researchers, clusters, SME-networks and public actors from different countries. The projects brought different expertise and perspectives together. These differences are an asset, they offer creative approaches that are needed to meet the great challenges addressed by StarDust.

To benchmark the innovation capacity in the Baltic Sea Region the BSR Innovation Monitor has been published in 2012, confirming that since 2006 the BSR is the only region which has seen an increasing innovation performance. To maintain and enhance this, a smart specialisation strategy is proposed.

4. Five subprojects

The five transnational projects are the core of StarDust

Comfort in Living

The partners in Comfort in Living are IDC West Sweden, the Art Academy of Latvia, the Business Cooperation Center of Southern Lithuania, and the Faculty of Wood Technology at the Poznan University of Life Science (Poland). The collaboration is developing transnational design and housing concepts for the needs of elderly people. Together the partners are planning a unique material library that is about to be established in Skövde in Sweden. It is the first material library of its kind in the Baltic Sea Region and it is an important element for the development of new products in the region.

Mobile Vikings

The Mobile Vikings project is about joining strong clusters and innovation milieus within Telecom/mobile applications into new ways of innovation activities. The purpose of this project is to leverage the industrial strongholds within the sector by implementing new methodologies and tools.

MarChain

The project MarChain connects the national maritime clusters in the Baltic Sea Region for increased competitiveness of the macro-region. The aim is to strengthen and improve the marine transport supply chains, efficiency and competitiveness. The project builds on cooperation between cluster initiatives around the Baltic Sea addressing issues such as environmentally friendly transport systems and intelligent ship, harbor and logistics solutions.

Active for Life

There is an increasing demand for new solutions that promote wellbeing and active ageing due to the ageing population in Europe. This is the point of departure for the StarDust project Active for Life. The aim is to create and provide innovative, globally competitive and effective trans-national service models and business concepts to maintain or improve the quality of life of the ageing population.

Clean Water

The vision of the Clean Water project is to create a vital Baltic Sea Region Clean Water Cluster, a cooperation platform of different clusters for interaction of all triple helix sectors in the BSR. The purpose of this platform is to develop water protection with new and innovative technologies, products and services.

14 I   Best practices

If you are interested to learn more about best practices please visit www.bsr-innovation.eu and navigate to"best practices". There you find an interactive map with links to outcomes and results.

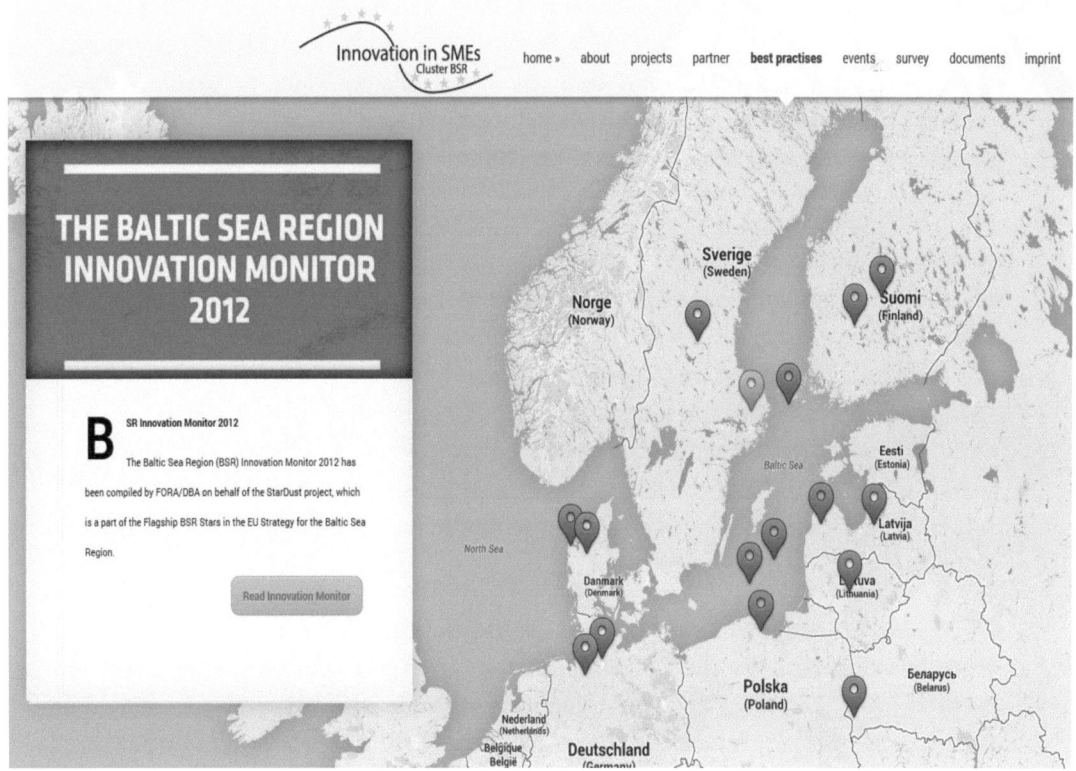

15 I   General reflections from the projects

Most project were implemented in three years. Considering a preparation, application and closure phase, experiences were gathered for four years. This section summarizes some of the projects general observations and lessons learned, that might be valuable for future projects.

Project Partnerships

All projects pointed out how important a good structured partnership is. This setup is crucial for the success or failure of a project. This holds true for the geographical distribution of the partners, but even more for the different professional backgrounds. The often called-for triple helix approach was considered as very useful, bringing together stakeholders with a background from business, academic and administration.

A clear communication between the partners is important. Every partner should be fully aware of his role and clearly contribute to the project. Often partners already knowing each other have a smoother implementation phase, at least if a core group of determined partners exists. Partners that joined projects in the last minute, just too have another partner from a specific, yet not covered country, often turned out to be more of burden for the remaining partners, that worked together on the application for a longer time. It has been noted, that the long running period of projects is helpful, since the trust building and getting to know each other takes several months alone.

Experienced project partners who have participated in several previous projects and are familiar with the administrative routine have been of advantage, although no new partners, who can bring new input to existing networks and cooperation's, should be excluded. A well-balanced partnership is a key factor for the success of a project.

Project Management

A strong project management is essential. One of the biggest overall challenges mentioned by most projects was the necessary working time spend for the administrative part of implementation: filling out activity and financial reports, time sheets, bookkeeping, controlling, auditing etc. A central, strong project management with the lead partner, that supported the partnership was very advantageous. Many projects made use of the "shared costs" possibility to implement a strong central project management while distributing the amount equally within the partnership.

Integration of SMEs

Like emphasized by many European funding programs. small and medium-sized enterprises are vital to an healthy economy and need the best possible support. The heavily funded FP7-Programme and it successor Horizon2020 exclusively dedicate a special amount to the financial promotion of SMEs. However, SMEs are a difficult target group to reach out to and often the dedicated amounts are not reached.

In this context a clear distinction must be made:

SMEs should and must be the beneficiaries of projects, not necessarily project partners. Reasons are rather simple and have also been confirmed in the survey 2013: the small firms lack the manpower to deal with the administrative work that comes with projects. Also, companies are not interested in three year running projects, but rather in fast, tangible solutions within a few weeks at most. The planning horizon of a SMEs is much shorter than that of an university or administration. While the PhD-students might plan three to four years for the dissertation on one topic, the owner of a company needs a solution as fast as possible..

The interest and needs of SMEs need to be bundled and facilitated by local or regional intermediate business organisations, that are connected to similar organisations in the Baltic Sea Region and are then able to compile and identify the needs, find solutions and transfer them back to the companies in their home region. Since trust is very important when joining forces with SMEs, it is good if the companies have a good working relation to those institutions.

Last but not least, the higher the level of specialisation and innovation of a company, the higher the risk is for participating companies to give knowledge to possible competitors in the same European market. Since the outcomes of publicly funded projects must be available to the public, companies are reluctant to share internal knowledge or develop patents without having the rights of intellectual property.

More flexible funding possibilities matching the needs from companies are needed. It would be a most welcome approach to find ways how to let more companies benefit not only from project results, but also from project funds, without burden them with the administrative work of a formal partner. This can be rather little and limited amounts. For example SMEs could be coached, trained, informed or simply invited to joint meetings, contribute with input, attend seminars, get reimbursement for travel costs etc. A solution could be to work with small lump sums.

The focus for all future project dealing with innovation in SMES should be, how much and how many companies are reached through the project results and in fact benefit from it. Too many solutions might look good in a report without reaching the companies in the region.

Financing for SMEs

Facilitating access to finance for SMEs is significant.. Numerous programs to provide financial funds to SMEs have been launched in the past[17] and will be launched for

---

[17] Supporting small and medium - sized enterprises in 2012 , A joint report of the European Commission and the EIB Group, available at
http://www.eif.org/news_centre/publications/joint_report_EIBGroup_EC_SMEs_access_to_finance.pdf

2014 – 2014, in particular by the EU programme for the Competitiveness of Enterprises and Small and Medium-sized Enterprises (SMEs) running from 2014 to 2020 with a planned budget of €2.3bn. The challenge is, that most SMEs cannot make use of these existing financial services. Larger, medium-sized companies with 100 – 200 employees usually have an in-house financial department to deal with the administrative work. The micro and small companies, who need the most financial support are simply overwhelmed with the applications and procedures. Thus those companies need a local contact to help them deal with the administrative work.

Pre-Financing

It turned out to be a challenge for several project partners to pre-finance their work. While many EU funded programs work with instalment or advance payments, this is yet not possible in the framework of INTERREG projects. The regular time period of pre-financing, from starting the work, submitting a project, clarify questions and receive the payment was between 9-13 months. For some project partners this can be very difficult. In a few cases project partners could only participate since stronger financial lead partners pre-financed some of the costs from their own funds and at their own risk. The obligatory pre-financing of the INTERREG projects is another reason, why it would be very difficult for small companies to join projects.

Flexibility

The long period of the projects results in a lack of flexibility. Between the moment a project is planned, an application filled out and the closure 4 years pass. Often something that has been considered important during the application is less relevant for the overall objective of the project or simply turned out not to be feasible. Since the project's success is always measured in the context of this application, this can be a challenge. However, in more severe cases of some projects that had to make bigger adjustments during project lifetime, it has been noted, that the responsible authority, in case of INTERREG the Joint Technical Secretariat, has been very supportive and constructive to find the best solution. It might be better to evaluate and judge projects on their success in realising the objective concrete results, rather on the method that was formulated in the application form

A performance-oriented planning and project implementation would also waive the detailed planning of all milestones for 3 - 4 years. Even though this makes controlling easier, it robs flexibility in the implementation of the project. The projects are simply not able to react to new developments, specific strengths of individual partners, region-specific characteristics, etc. The implementation of the projects thus no longer concentrates on the achievement of the best results, but on the compliance with the originally planned expenditure per activity or partner like written down in the application. However, it should be rather secondary, which partner when and how fulfil certain tasks, as long as these tasks are realised. Decisive factor should be that the partners reach the best possible result.

The award, execution and control of projects should be consistently success-oriented. It makes sense to agree and control the outputs, namely what outcome should be realised with a specific effort and actually has been achieved. It is less important whether it is personnel, equipment, or external cost. The decisive factor is whether the approved total costs were not exceeded and, in particular, whether the effort made stood om a reasonable proportion to the achieved result. Such a output-oriented approach is less about budget lines and work-packages. Important is the relation between effort (input) and outcome (output). Such an approach would increase the flexibility on how to achieve promised results, but increases the responsibility of the project for the success and financial risk. A project would be motivated to make every effort to realise the promised results (outputs) and to consider the costs (input) economically.

Sustainability

Projects funded with public money should always be the start of something new, that develops and life's on after the project ends. In most projects this has been the case. If the project develops methods or networks that correspond to an actual real need, they were able to continue and expand their work after project end. Also, many projects realised additional results. It might be an interesting idea from programmes perspective to award additional results after project end with a small lump sum, i.e. 5 % of project budget, and thus create a stimulus for projects to achieve more than they planned or promised.

A network of project partners may be active after the project ends. If partners continue to cooperate even after the funding of the project stopped, this can be especially fruitful. The building of a good-working network takes time. In this context it is very valuable that INTERREG funding allows for longer project periods of up to three years, at least a year longer than many other EU funded programs. This is beneficial to realise sustainable results.

Needs

To identify the real market needs of the targeted SMEs while developing a project should be imperative. At the core of the innovation ecosystem should be the precise product, process or organisational idea. This should be clearly demand driven and user focused. All the important fields that should be considered are arranged around that very idea in a circular manner signifying that they should be addressed in common and in an iterative fashion.

In few projects it turned out, that some results were far more important for the companies than others, that the partnership rated more important. An early involvement of SMEs or SME organisations is strongly recommended to make sure that the project tackles the real future needs. To learn more about the possible future needs, the cluster ran a survey in 2013.

2. Part: Survey 2013

1 I Introduction

To learn more about the innovation in SMEs in the respective countries in the Baltic Sea Region, learn from previous projects and identify the future needs, the cluster implemented an online survey that took place from March 2013 until August 2013.

The survey was programmed in way, that allows to draw conclusions for each group of participants, countries, group of countries or the Baltic Sea Region as a whole. This way, a comprehensive overview can be given. The survey used a piped logic system, i.e. the following question depended on previous answers. In case of multiple answers / ratings a random function was used to guarantee a balanced result.

The survey was rather demanding, since it took between 10 – 15 minutes to fill out. Nevertheless 608 participants completed the survey, allowing to draw a clear picture.

2 I Geographical coverage of participants

Overall 608 participants filled out the questionnaire until August 2013:

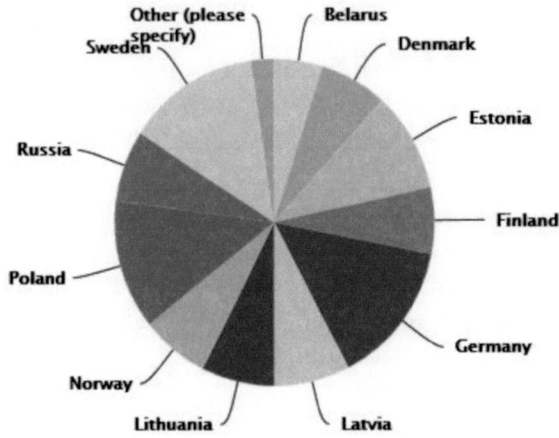

Answer Choices		Responses	
Belarus		4.93%	30
Denmark		6.74%	41
Estonia		9.87%	60
Finland		6.58%	40
Germany		14.31%	87
Latvia		7.57%	46
Lithuania		7.40%	45
Norway		6.91%	42
Poland		12.83%	78
Russia		7.07%	43
Sweden		13.49%	82
Other (please specify)	Responses	2.30%	14
Total			608

3 I Professional background

The participants were asked to inform about their professional background. 46.88 % of all surveyed represent the private business sector.

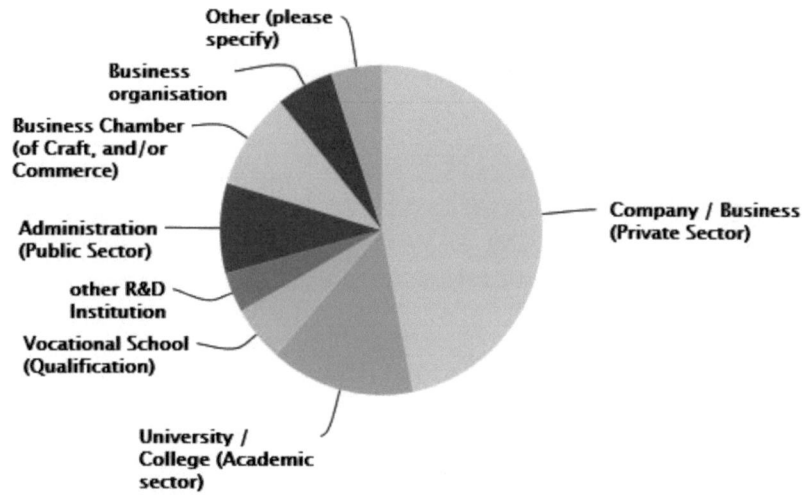

Answer Choices		Responses	
Company / Business (Private Sector)		46.88%	285
University / College (Academic sector)		14.47%	88
Vocational School (Qualification)		5.43%	33
other R&D Institution		3.95%	24
Administration (Public Sector)		8.88%	54
Business Chamber (of Craft, and/or Commerce)		9.54%	58
Business organisation		5.76%	35
other organisation		0%	0
Other (please specify)	Responses	5.10%	31
Total			608

4 I Participation of private companies

From the 285 private companies, 17,54 % were from Sweden, 13,68 % from Germany, 11,23 % from Estonia and 10,88 % from Poland. It must be noted, that these numbers do not reflect the total number of enterprises and population in the participating countries and cannot be extrapolated.

This is probably due to the language of the survey (English) and the background of the project partners.

A survey translated into the respective national languages would surely attend much more respondents, in particular from countries like Russia and Poland. Also the majority of project partners, in particular lead partners, came from Germany and Sweden and forwarded the survey in their networks, which accounts for a rather high participation from these countries.

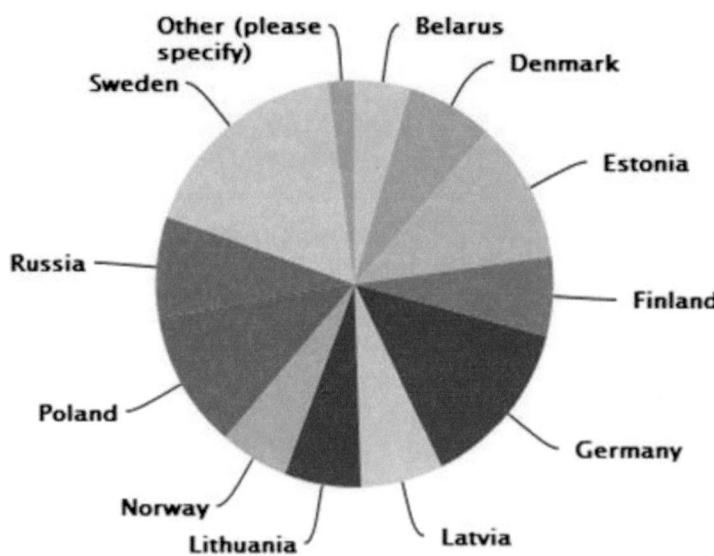

Answer Choices		Responses
Belarus		4.56%
Denmark		7.02%
Estonia		11.23%
Finland		6.32%
Germany		13.68%
Latvia		6.67%
Lithuania		6.32%
Norway		5.61%
Poland		10.88%
Russia		8.07%
Sweden		17.54%
Other (please specify)	Responses	2.11%

5 I Market range of participating companies

More than 75 % of all companies are active on a national or international market. This number is rather high, since most SMEs usually target only the regional market and have huge export potentials. It is likely, that many SMEs in the project networks are working on a national or international level.

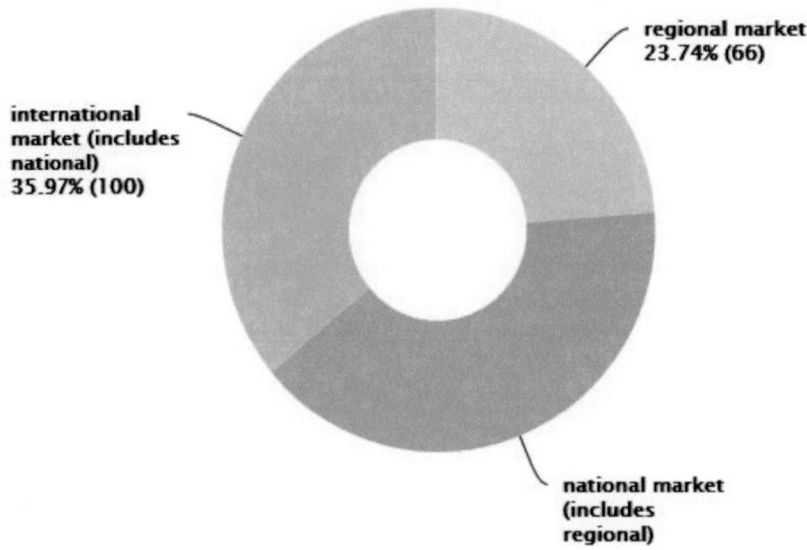

A differentiated analyses of the figures reveals, that innovative companies are more active on national and international markets, while non-innovative companies prefer the regional markets only.

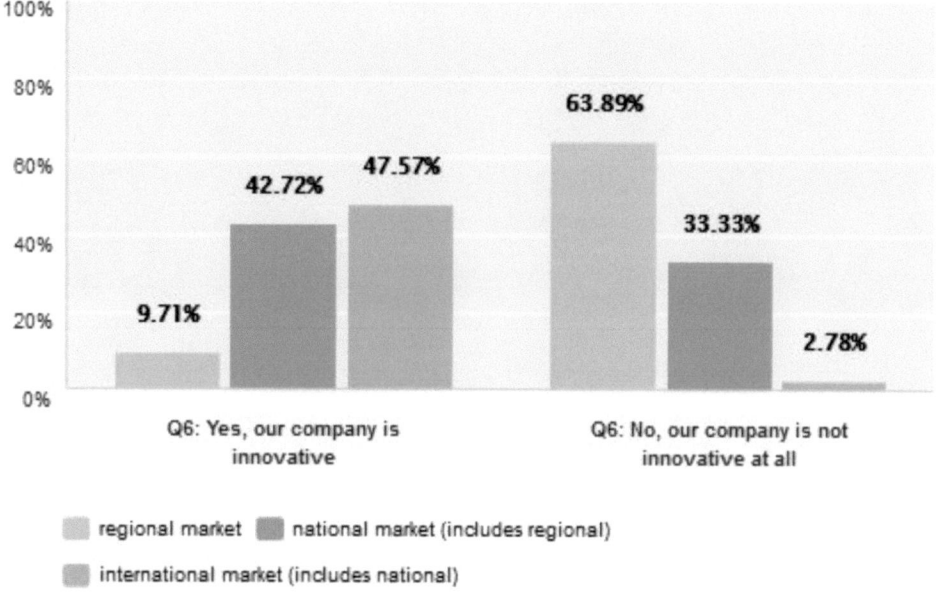

6 I Number of Employees

99,2 % of all companies in the Baltic Sea Region are SMEs, i.e. having less than 250 employees. The biggest share of these companies are the micro companies with less than 9 employees. This survey confirms this only partly, however more than 60 % of the surveyed companies have less than 9 employees.

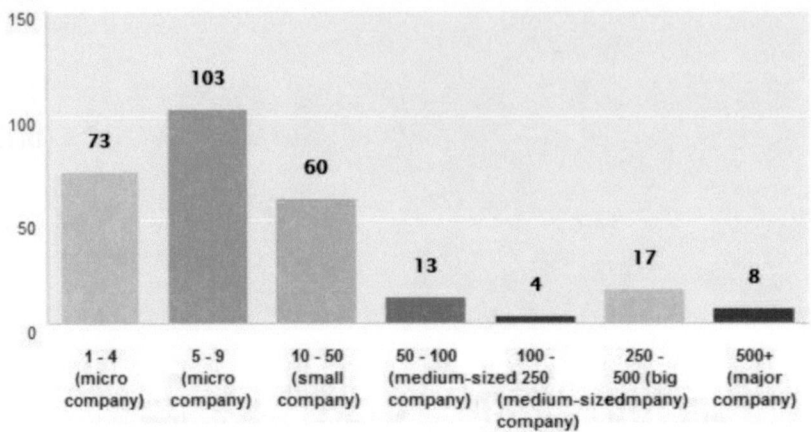

7 I Innovation level

Asked to self-evaluate the innovation level the majority of all companies clearly consider themselves innovative. This does not correspond to overall statistics and might be a result of many companies filling out the questionnaire, that benefited from one of the cluster projects and are innovative. Non-innovative companies are much harder to reach and refrain from participating in surveys.

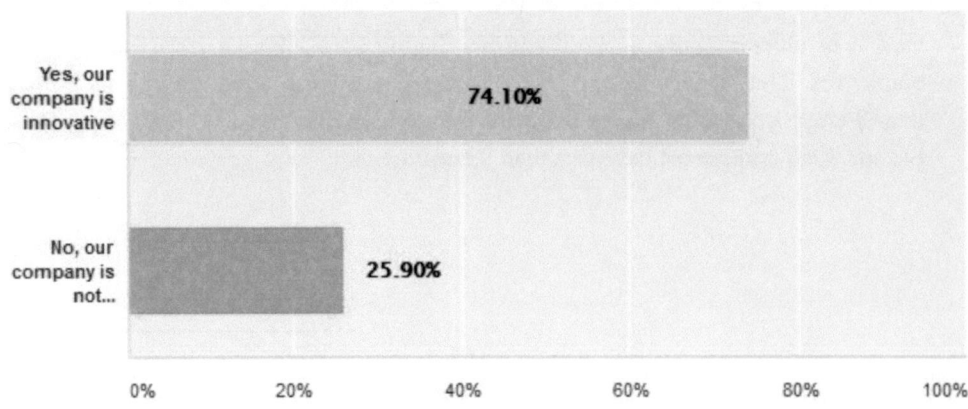

Broken down to each country, the numbers are quite different. It is evident, that companies from some countries, in particular northern regions like Sweden (91,84 %) or Denmark (90 %) consider themselves much more innovative, than southern countries like Poland (43,33 %) or Russia (34,78 %). This might indicate also a different self-confidence of the entrepreneurs in the respective countries.

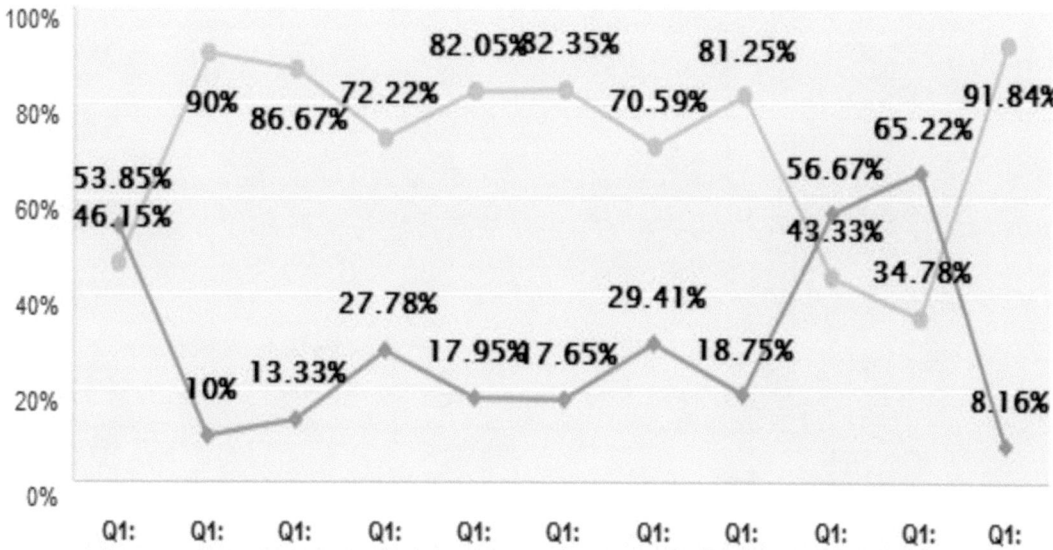

	Yes, our company is innovative	No, our company is not innovative at all
Q1: Belarus	46.15% 6	53.85% 7
Q1: Denmark	90% 18	10% 2
Q1: Estonia	86.67% 26	13.33% 4
Q1: Finland	72.22% 13	27.78% 5
Q1: Germany	82.05% 32	17.95% 7
Q1: Latvia	82.35% 14	17.65% 3
Q1: Lithuania	70.59% 12	29.41% 5
Q1: Norway	81.25% 13	18.75% 3
Q1: Poland	43.33% 13	56.67% 17
Q1: Russia	34.78% 8	65.22% 15
Q1: Sweden	91.84% 45	8.16% 4

8 I Kind of Innovations

Those companies who considered themselves innovative were asked to further inform about the nature of their innovations, rating from 1 (not innovative) to 5 (highly innovative). The majority of companies is innovative in the field of product innovations, followed by service innovations. A clear gap exists towards the organisational innovations.

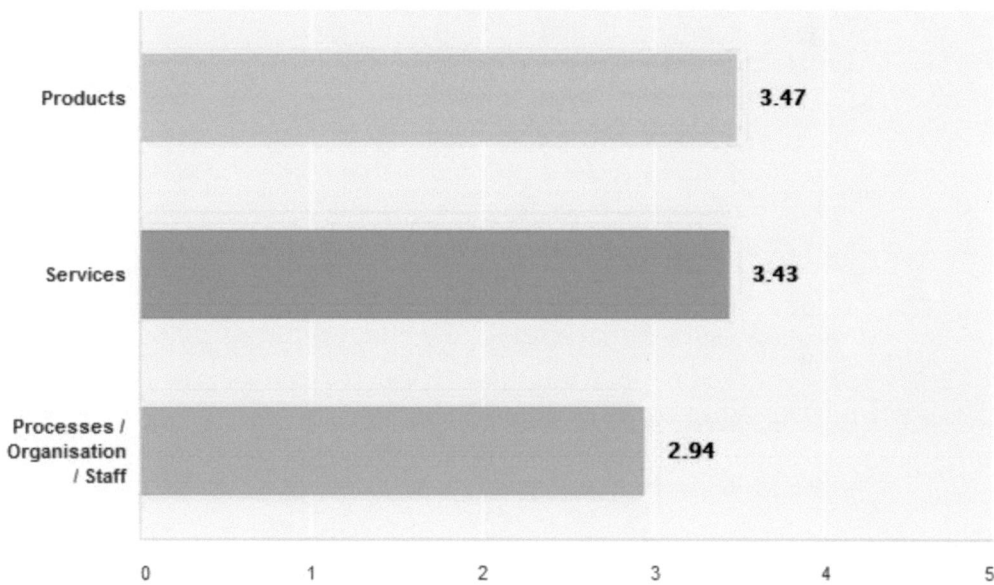

a. Product Innovation level per country

Taking a look at the country specific innovation levels indicates that German, Estonian and Swedish companies are rather strong when it comes to product innovation.

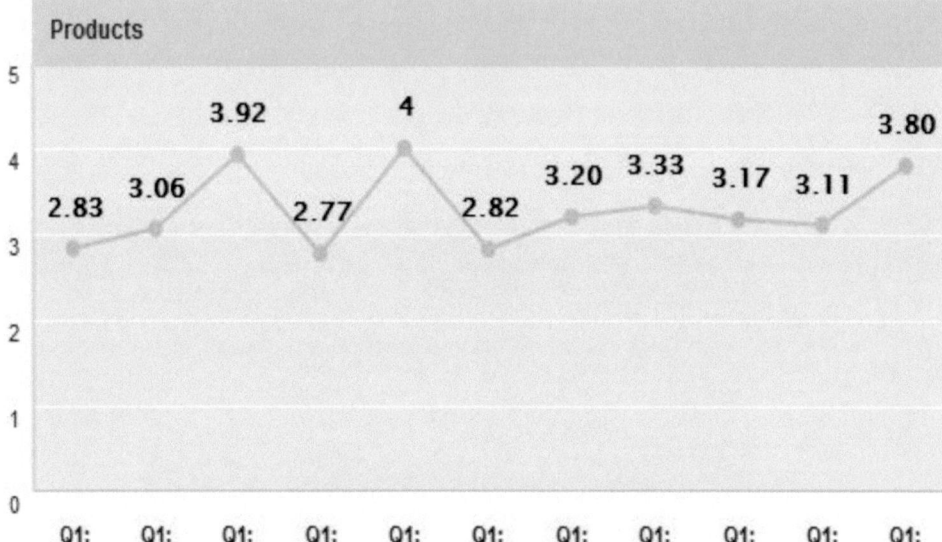

b. Services Innovation level per country

Service innovations are in particular high in Sweden and Lithuania.

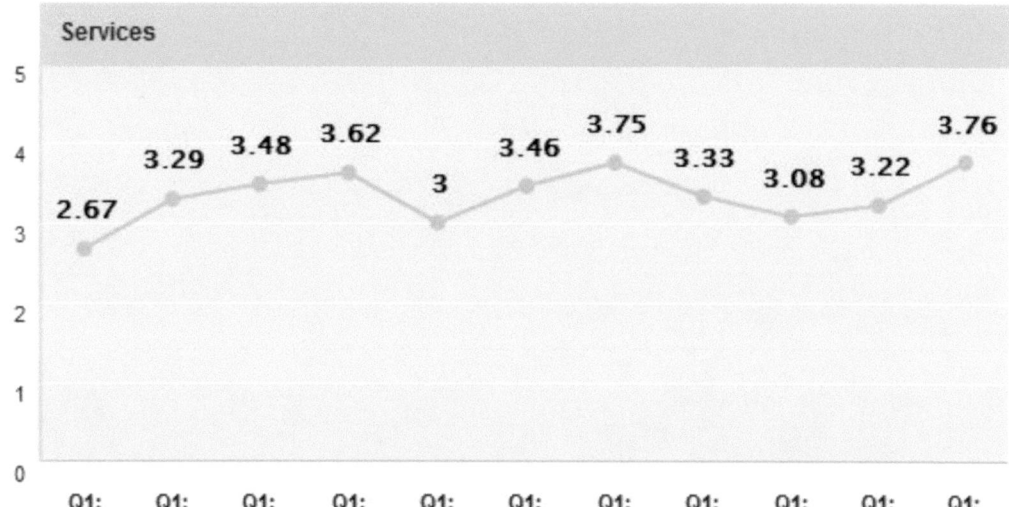

c. Organisational Innovation level per country

The rather less well-known organizational innovations, the way companies work, internal cooperation between employees, methods like lean management etc. are hardly exploited. Here the biggest gaps are evident, for example very low levels in countries with a traditional hierarchic, top-to-bottom structure, like Belarus, Poland and Russia, while a much higher level in Estonia or Sweden. Social Trust is a very important indicator for a well-working society[18], and also very important for the way people work together. Sweden is worldwide on of the countries with the highest level of trust[19]. It is therefore consequent, that in this region most organizational innovations find a fruitful soil.

---

[18] Social Trust in Seven Nations, http://www.econstor.eu/bitstream/10419/50209/1/350527032.pdf
[19] http://www.pewglobal.org/2008/04/15/where-trust-is-high-crime-and-corruption-are-low/ or http://www.jdsurvey.net/jds/jdsurveyMaps.jsp?Idioma=I&SeccionTexto=0404&NOID=104

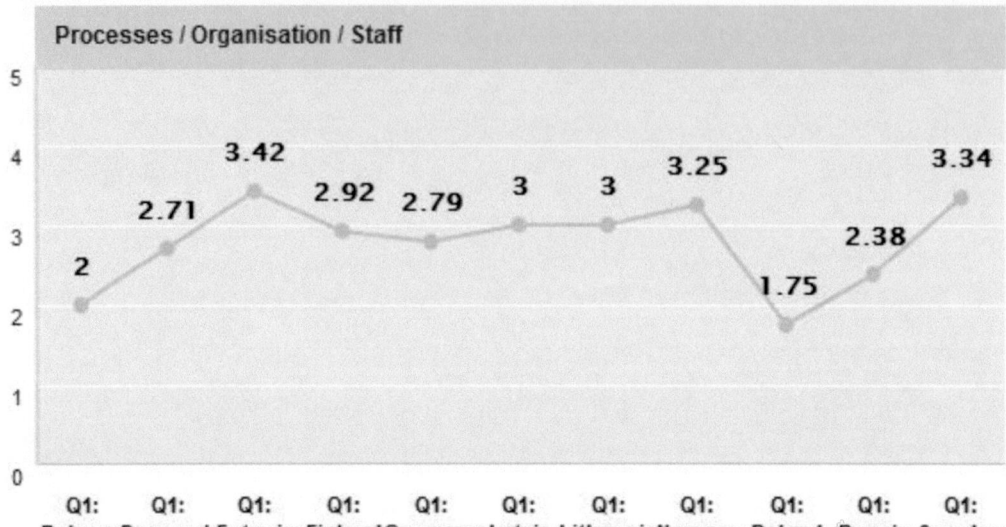

9 I Being Innovative to stay competitive

Asked if being innovative is an important element to stay competitive, the companies affirmed this with a vast majority of 78,28 %, while 21,21 % believe that being innovative might not be essential for a company to stay in business and grow, but helpful. Only 0,51 % stated that innovation is not a prerequisite for competitiveness.

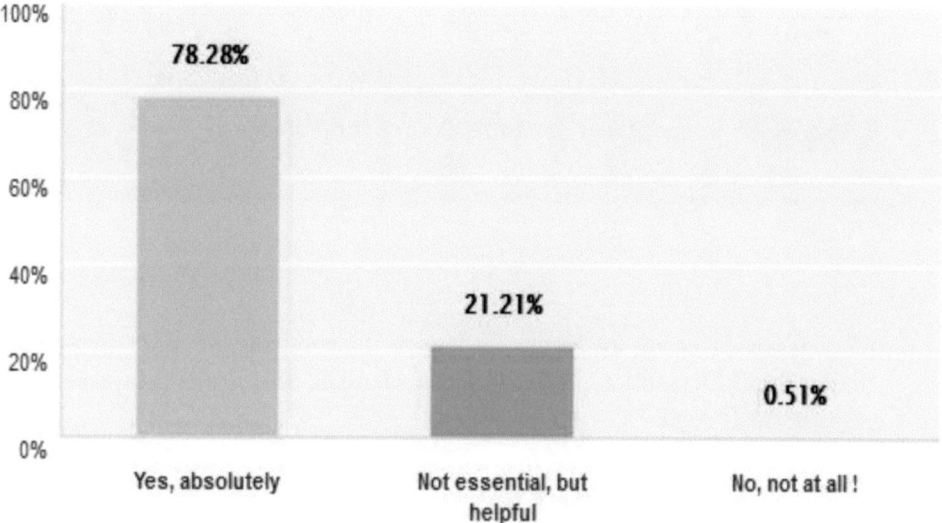

10 I   R&D activities of companies

The innovative companies have been asked, if they are engaged in research and development activities and if so, to what extent. Most companies were not engaged in R&D of their own, only very few have a R&D department.

1 (no R&D)	2	3 (some R&D)	4	5 (own R&D department)
35.96%	11.33%	24.14%	10.34%	18.23%
73	23	49	21	37

As could be expected, the bigger the size of the company, the more likely it is to operate a R&D Department. The majority of small- and micro companies is not engaged in R&D at all.

	1 (no R&D)	2	3 (some R&D)	4	5 (own R&D department)
Q5: 1 - 4 (micro company)	34.15% 14	14.63% 6	26.83% 11	9.76% 4	14.63% 6
Q5: 5 - 9 (micro company)	54.79% 40	4.11% 3	17.81% 13	9.59% 7	13.70% 10
Q5: 10 - 50 (small company)	20.41% 10	26.53% 13	28.57% 14	8.16% 4	16.33% 8
Q5: 50 - 100 (medium-sized company)	41.67% 5	0% 0	33.33% 4	25% 3	0% 0
Q5: 100 - 250 (medium-sized company)	50% 2	0% 0	0% 0	0% 0	50% 2
Q5: 250 - 500 (big company)	5.88% 1	5.88% 1	41.18% 7	5.88% 1	41.18% 7
Q5: 500+ (major company)	14.29% 1	0% 0	0% 0	28.57% 2	57.14% 4

11 I Spending for R&D activities

Those companies, which are engaged in R&D activities, were asked about the amount they invest, based on their total budget. Most innovative companies that are doing R&D on their own clearly invest more than 10 % of their budget, showing the importance of R&D.

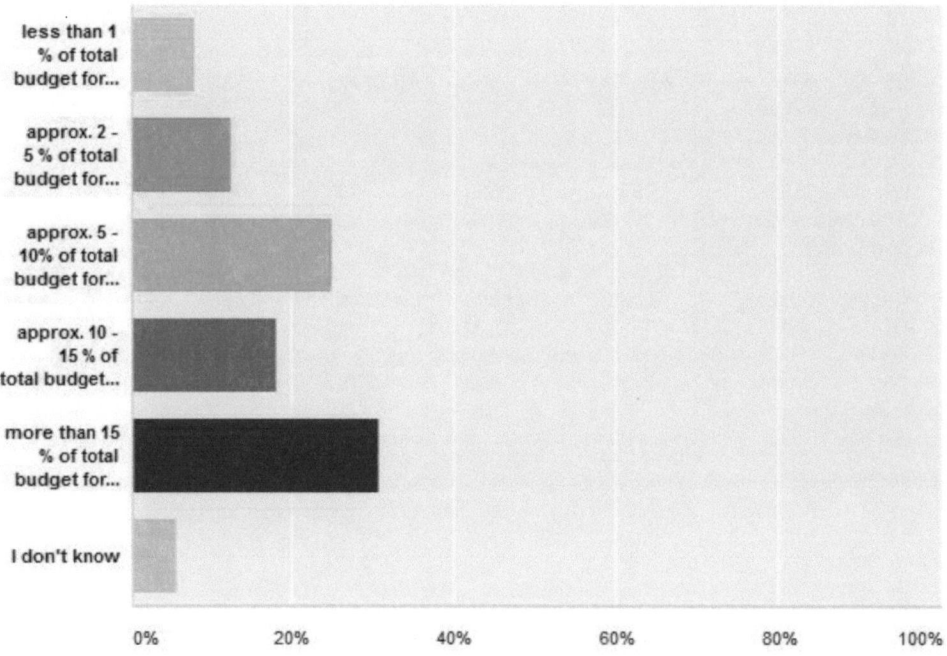

12 I Average Innovation level of organisations for different countries

Organisation, that are not SMEs, where asked to rate their level of innovation. The lowest average level indicated organisations from Russia (2,28) and Belarus (2.47). The highest average level was marked by organisations from

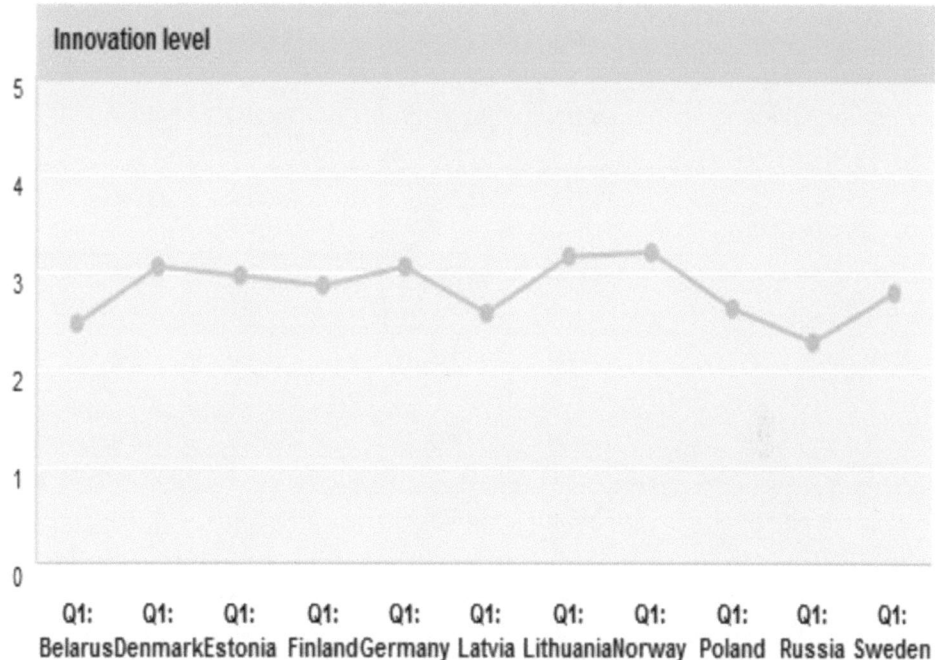

Innovation level	1 (not innovative)	2	3 (some innovations)	4	5 (Very innovative)
Q1: Belarus	20% 3	33.33% 5	33.33% 5	6.67% 1	6.67% 1
Q1: Denmark	10% 2	20% 4	35% 7	25% 5	10% 2
Q1: Estonia	16% 4	12% 3	36% 9	32% 8	4% 1
Q1: Finland	4.55% 1	36.36% 8	36.36% 8	13.64% 3	9.09% 2
Q1: Germany	15.91% 7	18.18% 8	31.82% 14	13.64% 6	20.45% 9
Q1: Latvia	11.54% 3	30.77% 8	46.15% 12	11.54% 3	0% 0
Q1: Lithuania	12% 3	12% 3	32% 8	36% 9	8% 2
Q1: Norway	4% 1	24% 6	28.00% 7	36% 9	8% 2
Q1: Poland	23.68% 9	18.42% 7	34.21% 13	18.42% 7	5.26% 2
Q1: Russia	38.89% 7	16.67% 3	22.22% 4	22.22% 4	0% 0
Q1: Sweden	14.29% 4	28.57% 8	28.57% 8	21.43% 6	7.14% 2

13 I   Innovation level per type of organisation

The innovation level for the participating types of organisation is very different. It comes with no surprise, that universities consider themselves most innovative, while business organisations or chambers operate rather traditional.

Innovation level					
	1 (not innovative)	2	3 (some innovations)	4	5 (Very innovative)
Q2: University / College (Academic sector)	5.19% 4	16.88% 13	40.26% 31	27.27% 21	10.39% 8
Q2: Vocational School (Qualification)	34.38% 11	50% 16	6.25% 2	3.13% 1	6.25% 2
Q2: other R&D Institution	0% 0	0% 0	45.45% 10	45.45% 10	9.09% 2
Q2: Administration (Public Sector)	25% 12	12.50% 6	43.75% 21	18.75% 9	0% 0
Q2: Business Chamber (of Craft, and/or Commerce)	30.19% 16	24.53% 13	26.42% 14	13.21% 7	5.66% 3
Q2: Business organisation	5.88% 2	29.41% 10	29.41% 10	32.35% 11	2.94% 1

14 I   Cooperation level with SMEs per type of organisation

Based on a rating from 1 (no contact) to 5 (close cooperation), the participants were asked to indicate their cooperation with SMEs.

Vocational schools, traditionally qualifying SME personnel, showed a very high average level of cooperation, followed by Chambers of Crafts and Commerce, that represent SMEs.

Remarkable was the fact, that so far R&D institutions indicated a lower level of cooperation with SMEs than public administrations.

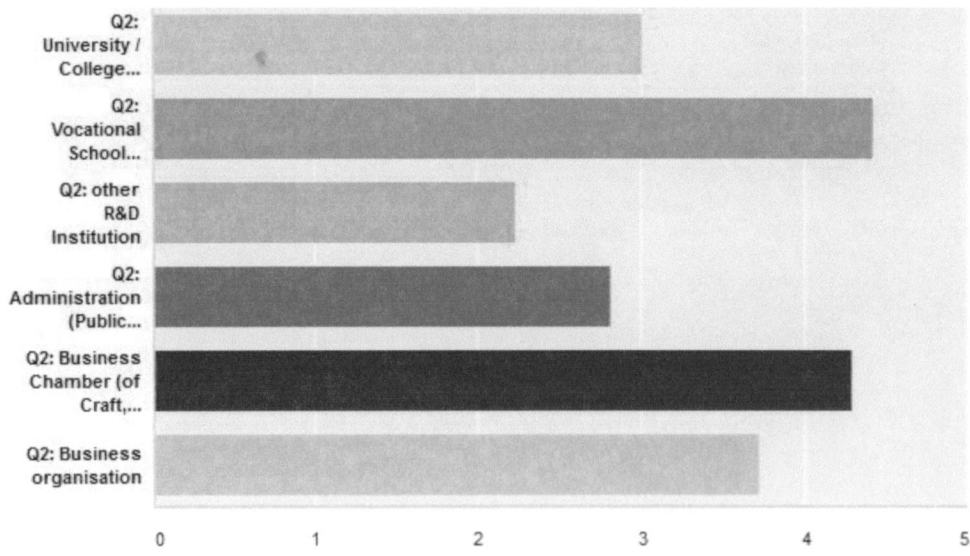

	1 No contact at all	2	3 some cooperation	4	5 close cooperation
Q2: University / College (Academic sector)	12.99% 10	19.48% 15	32.47% 25	24.68% 19	10.39% 8
Q2: Vocational School (Qualification)	6.25% 2	0% 0	9.38% 3	15.63% 5	68.75% 22
Q2: other R&D Institution	31.82% 7	40.91% 9	9.09% 2	9.09% 2	9.09% 2
Q2: Administration (Public Sector)	25% 12	18.75% 9	22.92% 11	16.67% 8	16.67% 8
Q2: Business Chamber (of Craft, and/or Commerce)	0% 0	3.77% 2	18.87% 10	22.64% 12	54.72% 29
Q2: Business organisation	0% 0	20.59% 7	20.59% 7	26.47% 9	32.35% 11

15 I   Cooperation level with SMEs by countries

Highest average cooperation level with SMEs per organisation is in Estonia (3,76), Finland (3,73), Denmark (3,65) Germany (3,64). A rather low average level is evident in Poland Russia (2,65), Poland (3,26) and Latvia (3,12).

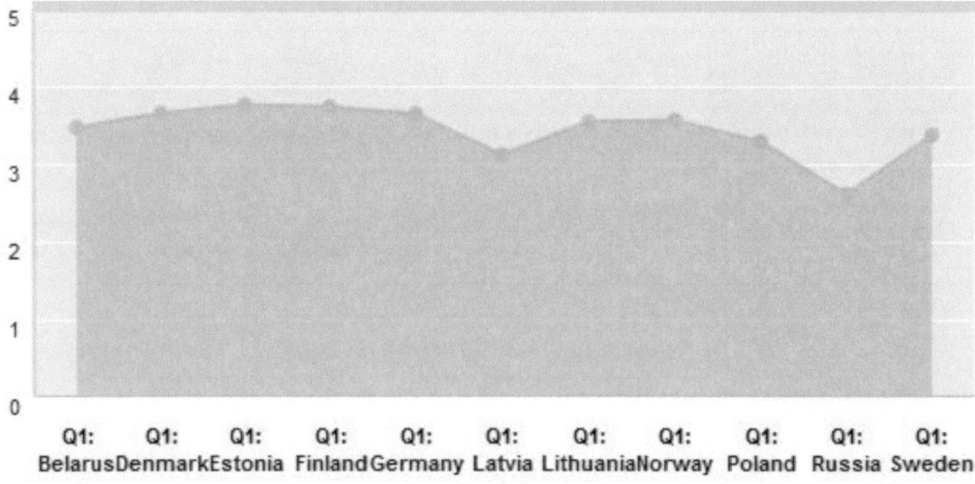

	1 No contact at all	2	3 some cooperation	4	5 close cooperation
Q1: Belarus	6.67% 1	26.67% 4	13.33% 2	20% 3	33.33% 5
Q1: Denmark	5% 1	25% 5	15% 3	10% 2	45% 9
Q1: Estonia	8% 2	8% 2	20% 5	28.00% 7	36% 9
Q1: Finland	13.64% 3	13.64% 3	4.55% 1	22.73% 5	45.45% 10
Q1: Germany	9.09% 4	9.09% 4	27.27% 12	18.18% 8	36.36% 16
Q1: Latvia	11.54% 3	19.23% 5	30.77% 8	23.08% 6	15.38% 4
Q1: Lithuania	7.69% 2	0% 0	42.31% 11	30.77% 8	19.23% 5
Q1: Norway	12% 3	16% 4	8% 2	32% 8	32% 8
Q1: Poland	7.89% 3	21.05% 8	31.58% 12	13.16% 5	26.32% 10
Q1: Russia	27.78% 5	33.33% 6	11.11% 2	5.56% 1	22.22% 4
Q1: Sweden	14.81% 4	11.11% 3	18.52% 5	33.33% 9	22.22% 6

16 I   Advantages of SMEs

The participants agree to a high majority with the statements claiming the advantages of small and medium sized enterprises

	No, not true	I don't know	Yes, true	Total
Small size = flexible, swift response times to market development	16.20% 81	16.40% 82	67.40% 337	500
Management by owner = short and direct decision making	3.61% 18	7.82% 39	88.58% 442	499
Low hierarchy = direct involvement and motiviation of staff	5.42% 27	13.25% 66	81.33% 405	498
Customer focused = close to market needs	15.26% 76	15.26% 76	69.48% 346	498
Cost-effective structures = smaller overhead costs, lower costs of innovation	30.92% 154	33.13% 165	35.94% 179	498

Companies that consider themselves innovative rated rather positive and agreed to the statements, compared to non-innovative firms:

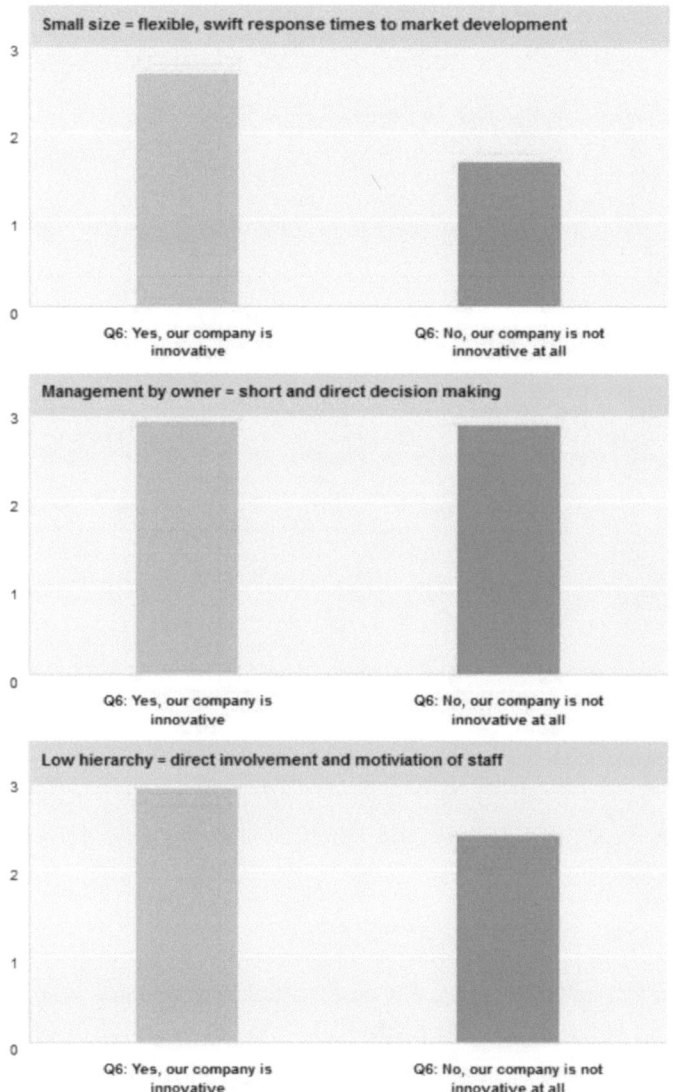

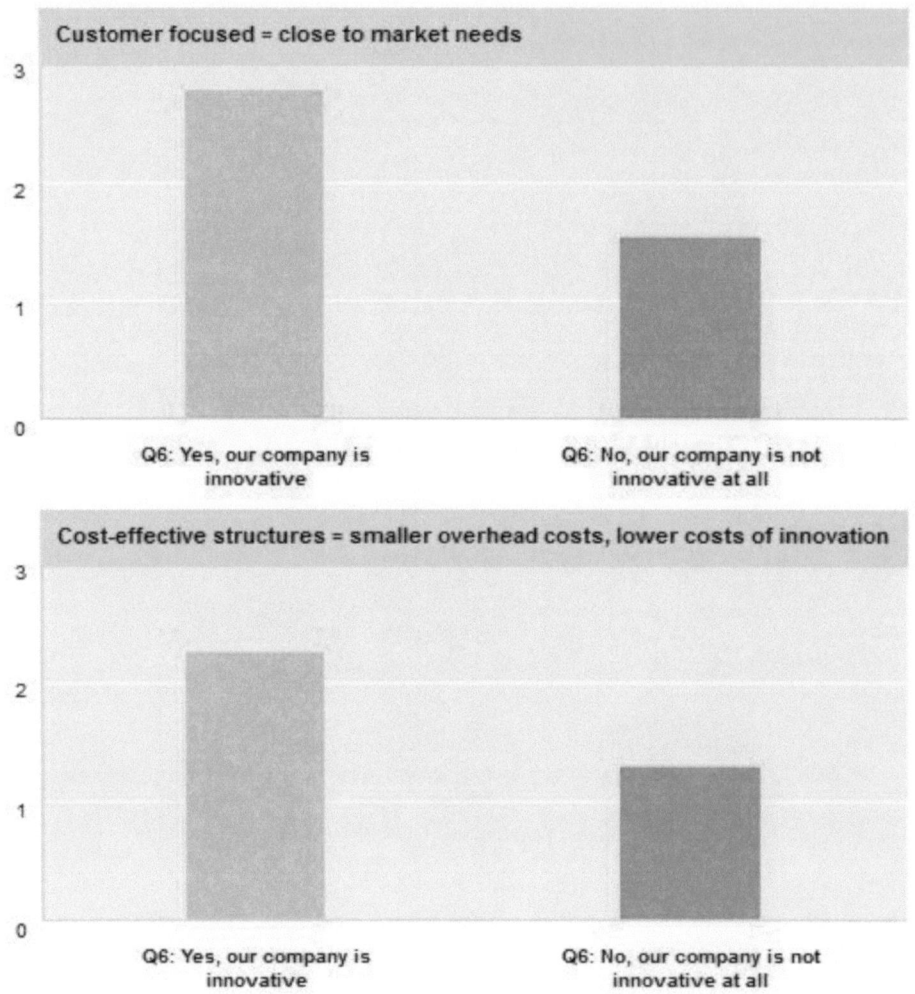

It can be concluded, that the advantages are not clear to those companies, who are not innovative. It has been commented, that many SMEs are not aware of these advantages and need support to discover them for their benefit.

17 I   Disadvantages of SMEs

To a large extent, the statements stating the disadvantages of SMEs were confirmed.

	No, not true	I don't know	Yes, true
Financing, undersized project portfolio= difficult to balance the economic risk.	9.58% 48	26.35% 132	64.07% 321
Lack of qualification = no qualifications that match SME needs	19.24% 96	18.24% 91	62.53% 312
Personnel = SMEs lack the number of skilled workers needed to realize innovations.	13.88% 69	12.88% 64	73.24% 364
Lack of information and knowledge =SMEs are often undersupplied with information.	34.47% 172	25.65% 128	39.88% 199

Innovative companies vs. non-innovative companies

Companies that consider themselves innovative rated quite similar to non-innovative firms. The lack of skilled workforce and adequate qualifications seems to be more evident in non-innovative companies:

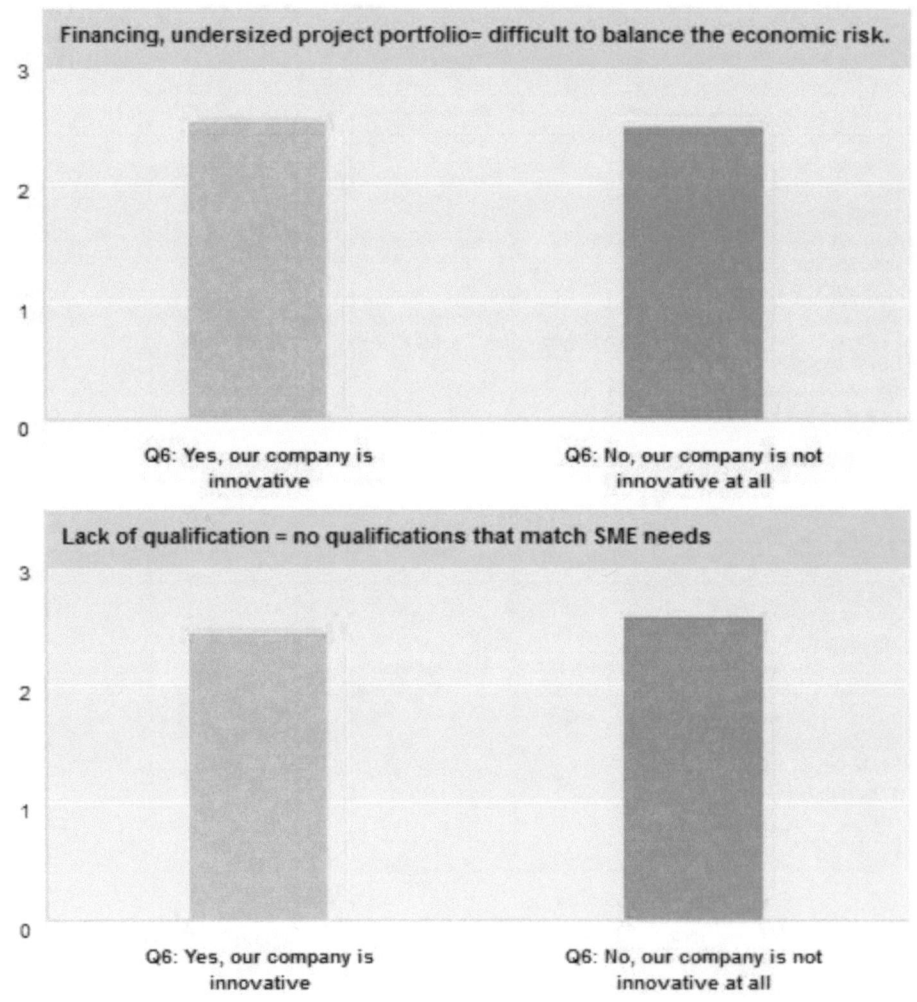

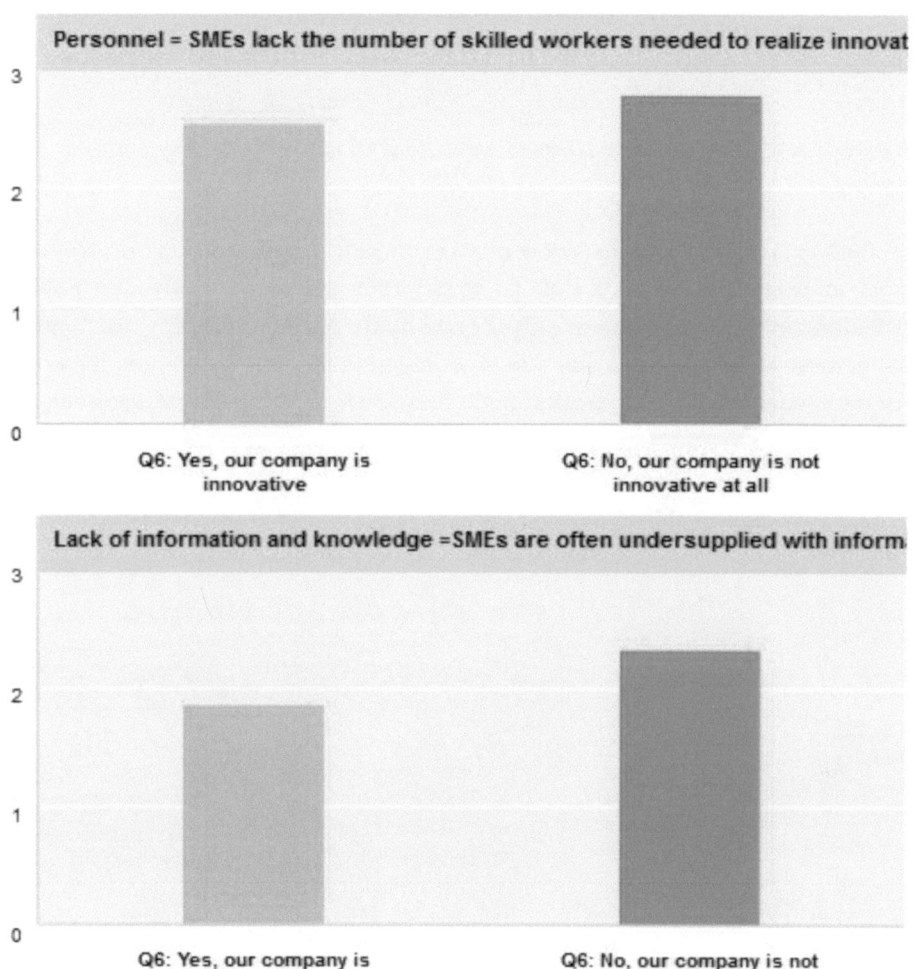

18 I   What kind of innovations are needed ?

The participants were asked to indicate, what kind of innovations they consider most important.

A product innovation refers to a new or a significantly improved good or service. A process innovation refers to a new or significantly improved production process, distribution method, marketing or support activity for goods or services. An organisational innovation refers to the way you work together in a company, how the potential of every employee is used, work climate, innovative thinking of managers etc.

The average results of all participants is almost even.

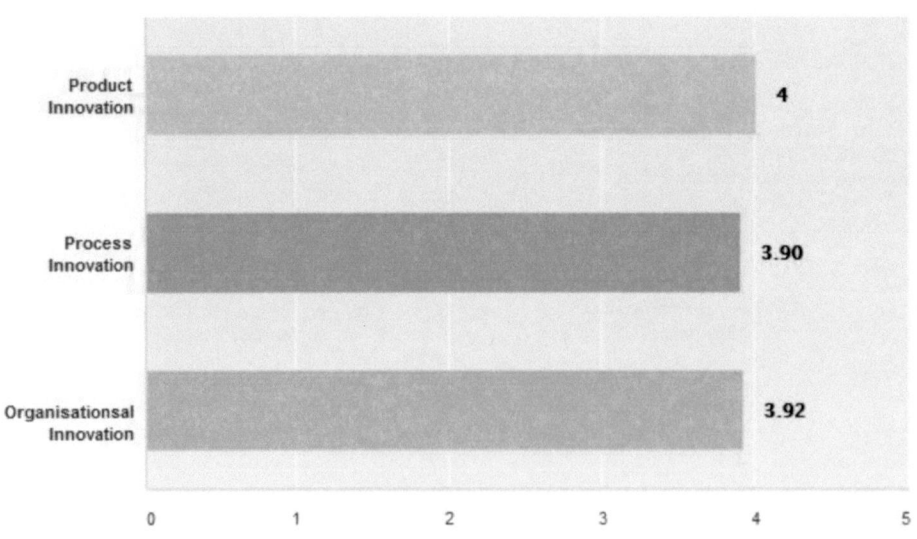

19 I   Kind of innovations asked for per country

Analysing the answers per country, show that product innovations are much more asked for in countries like Belarus, Poland and Russia. Nordic countries like Denmark, Norway and Sweden expressed a much higher interest in process/service and organizational innovations in SMEs.

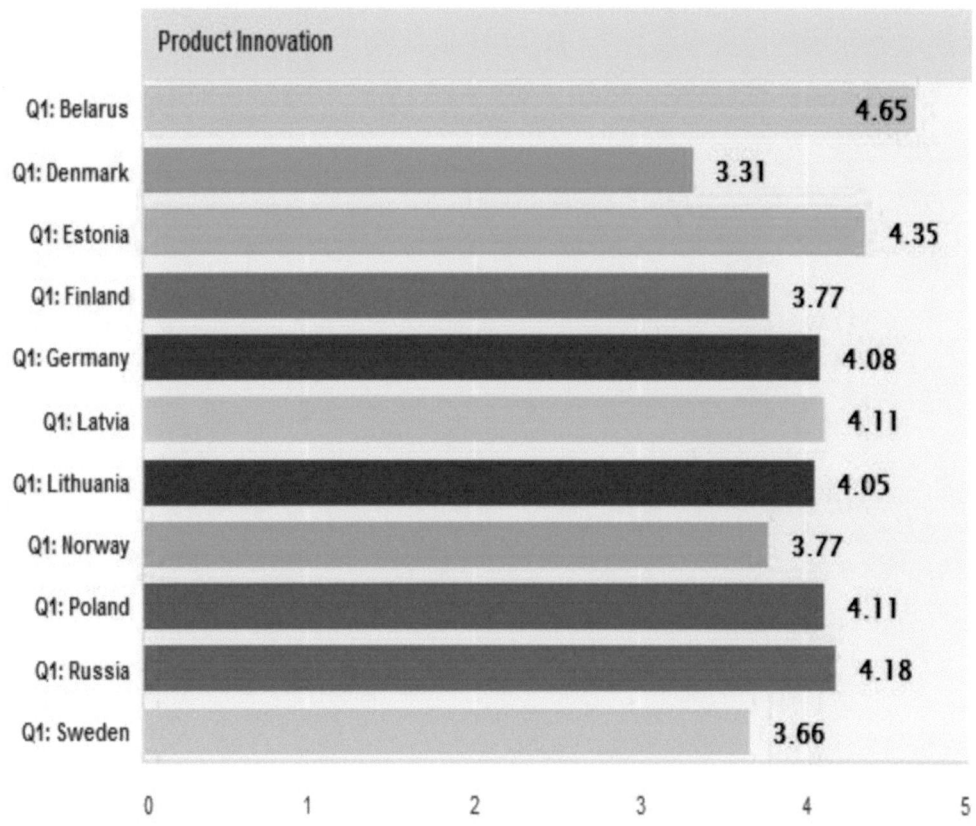

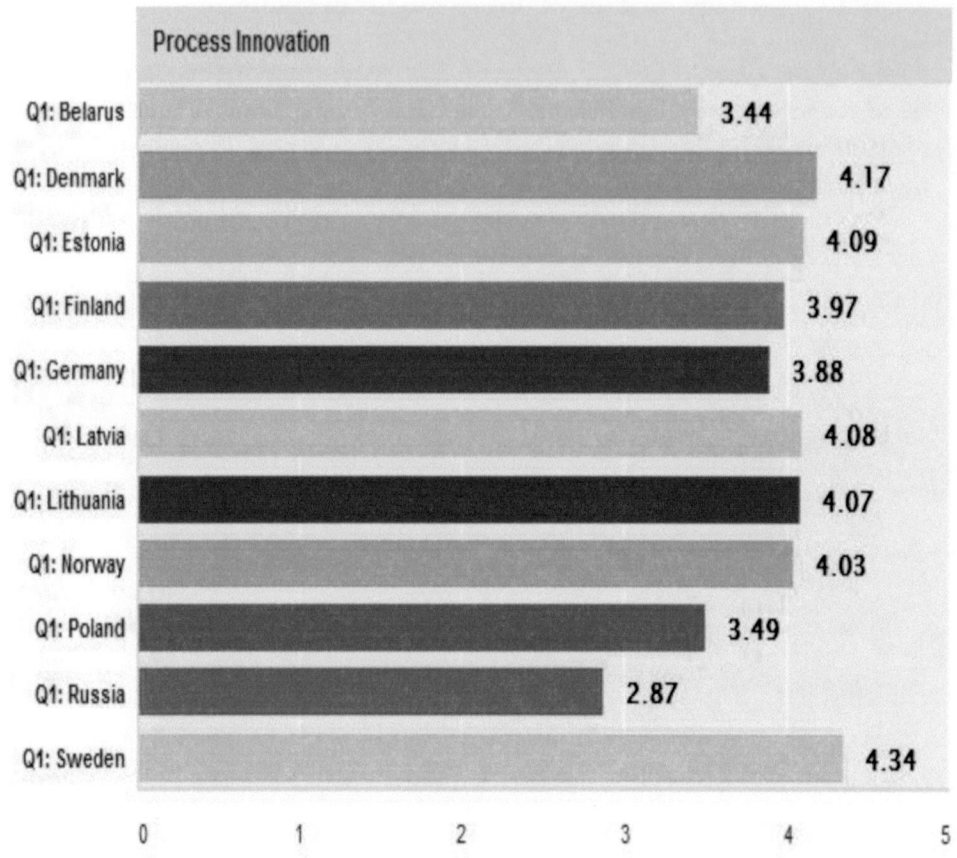

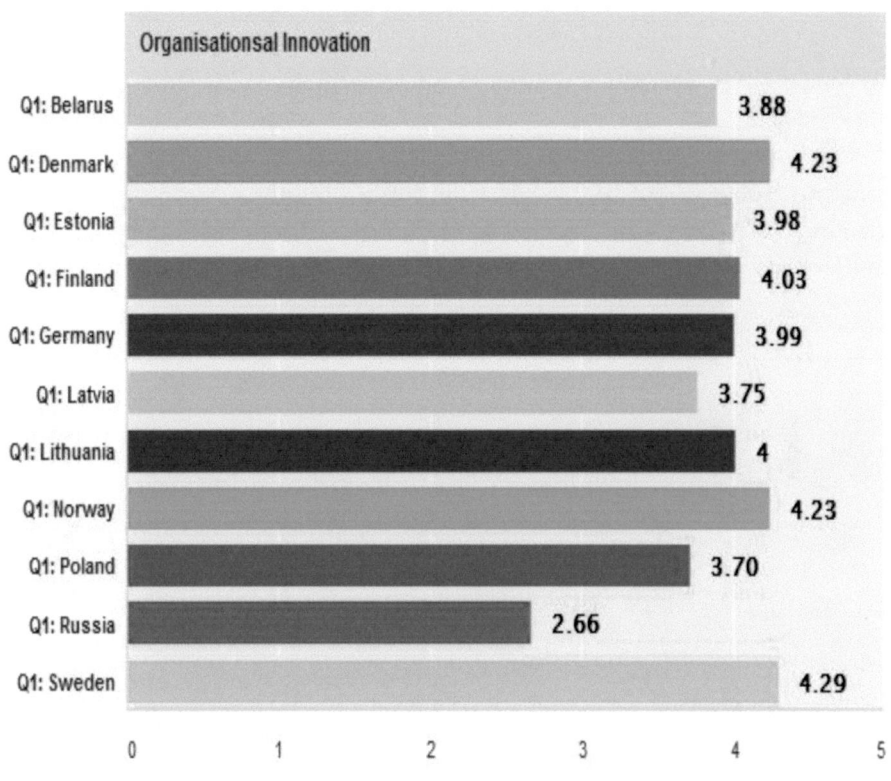

20 I   Kind of innovations asked for per group of participants

Revealing are also the different answers for each group of participants. Universities and Colleges see the highest need in process and organizational innovations, which correspond to their main activity , education. Pure R&D institutions and companies underline the importance of Product innovations . Business chambers and other organisations have a slight preference for process and organizational innovations. Public administrations rate all three kind of innovations of equal importance.

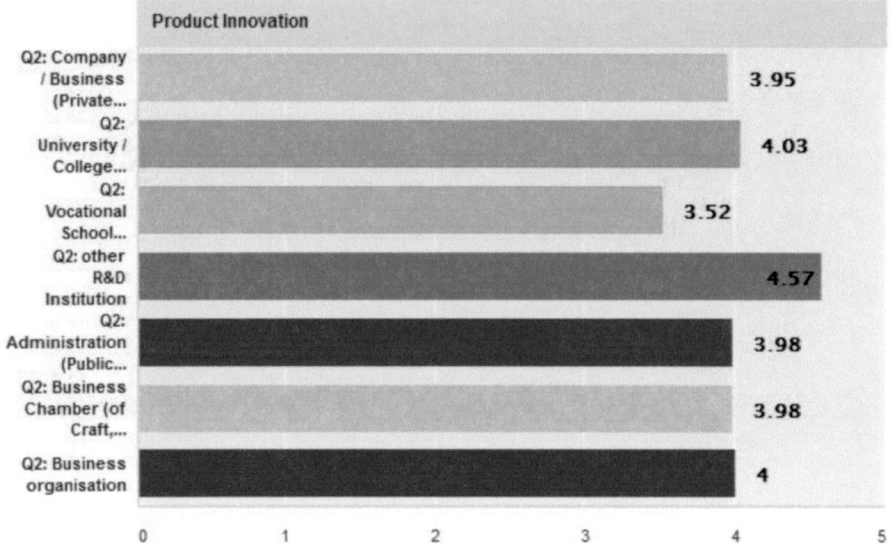

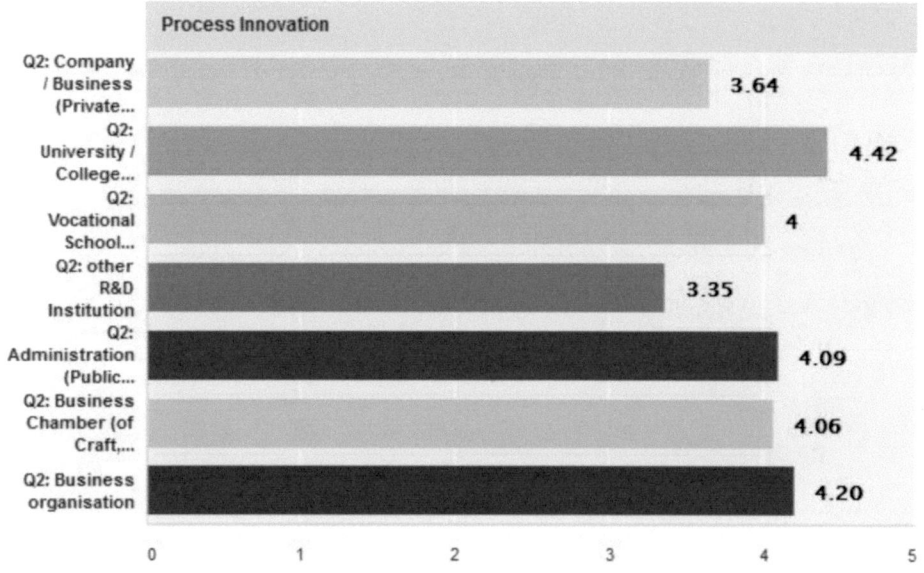

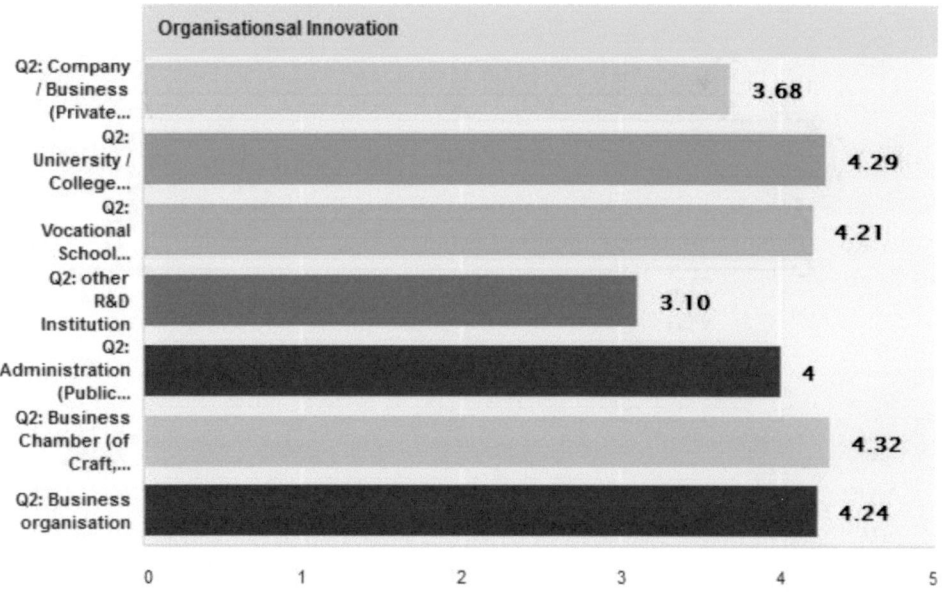

21 I   Cooperation of SMEs with

SMEs have the strongest cooperation with vocational schools and chambers.

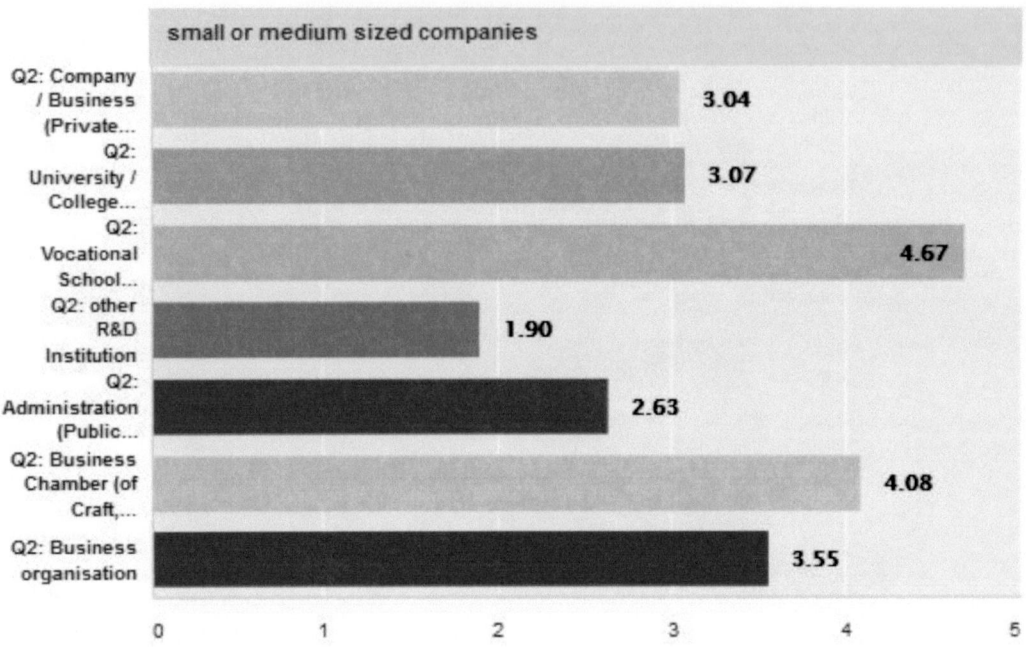

22 I   Cooperation of big companies with

Big companies have a rather close cooperation with universities and business organisations.

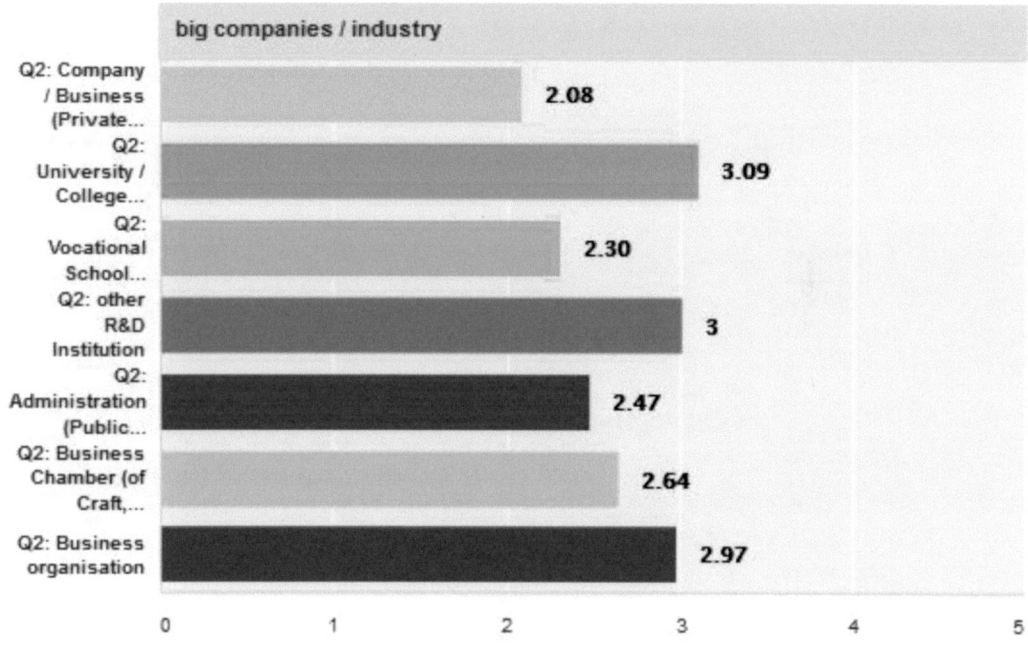

23 I   Cooperation of public administrations with

Public administrations indicated the highest level of cooperation with other administrations, followed by universities and Chambers.

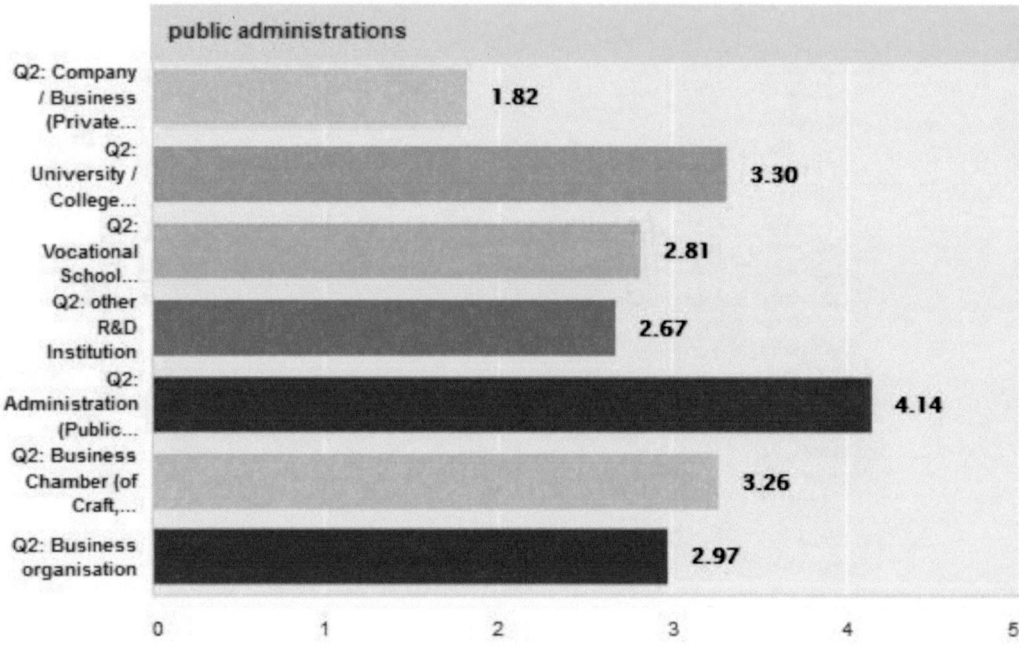

24 I   Cooperation of Chambers / Business Organisations with

Chambers and Business organisations have a high level of cooperation with vocational schools (that are often embodied in the chambers) and other chambers and administrations.

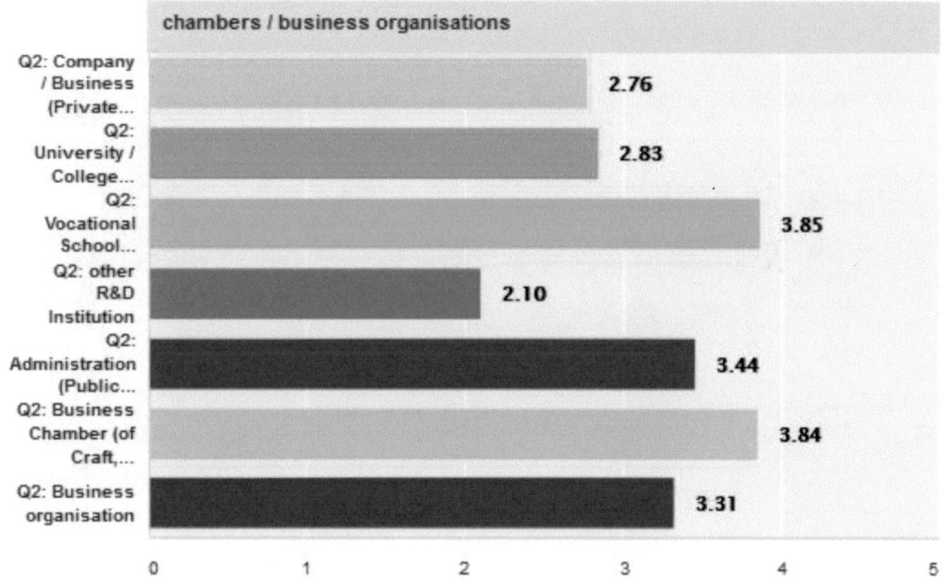

25 I   Cooperation of Universities/Schools with

Universities if a rather low level of cooperation with SMEs, but high level of cooperation with other universities/Colleges. Usually universities are well connected with
each other, on national and international level.

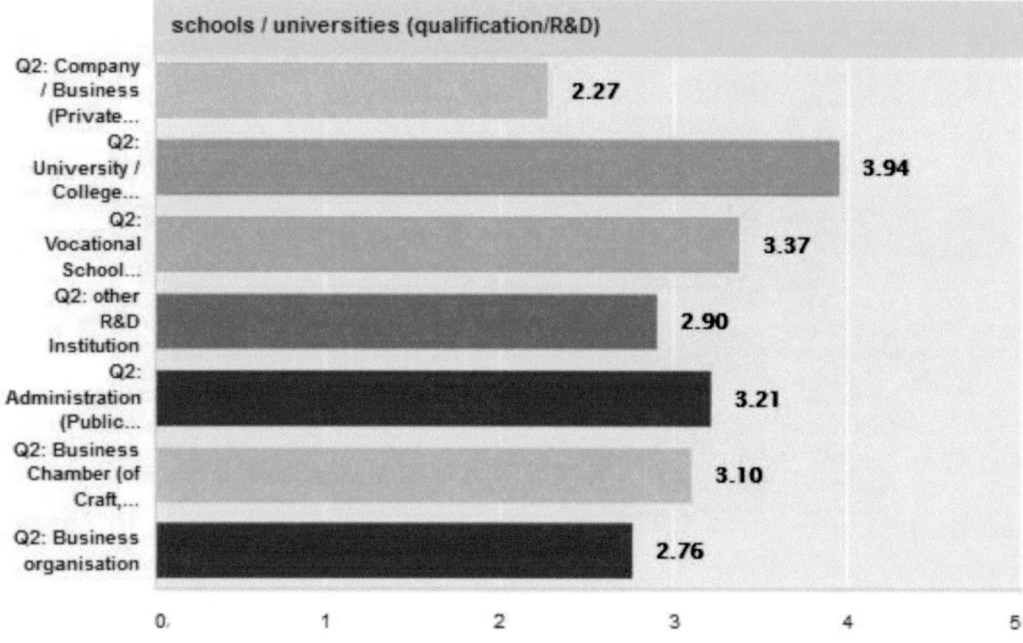

26 I   Cooperation of Technology Parks/Incubators with

Technology Parks have overall the lowest level of cooperation and since they are often initiated by administrations the highest level of cooperation with this group.

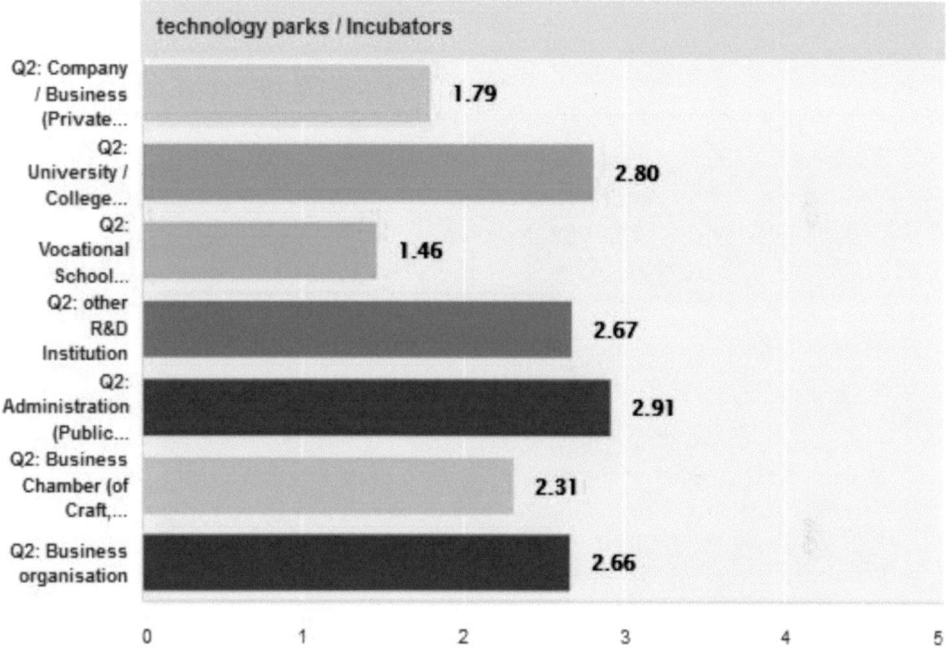

27 I   Activity in international innovation projects

The participants were asked to indicate, if they have been active in projects. The overall number is rather high, but due to the fact that the survey was communicated in a network of projects, not a surprise.

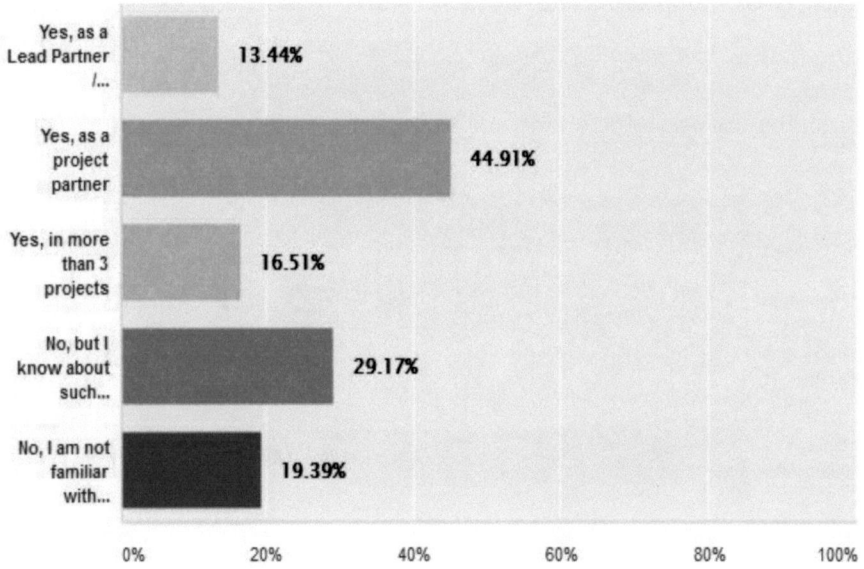

28 I   Participation of SMEs in innovation projects

Often it has been discussed, if SMEs should directly be eligible as project partners. In some European Funding Schemes like the 7th Research Framework Program this was possible, in most ERDF funded Programmes like INTERREG IV B private companies could not be part of a partnership.

Asked, if SMEs should be able to become part of a project, the majority of participants (58,14 %) thought that the interests of SMEs should be presented more, but not SMEs directly partners.

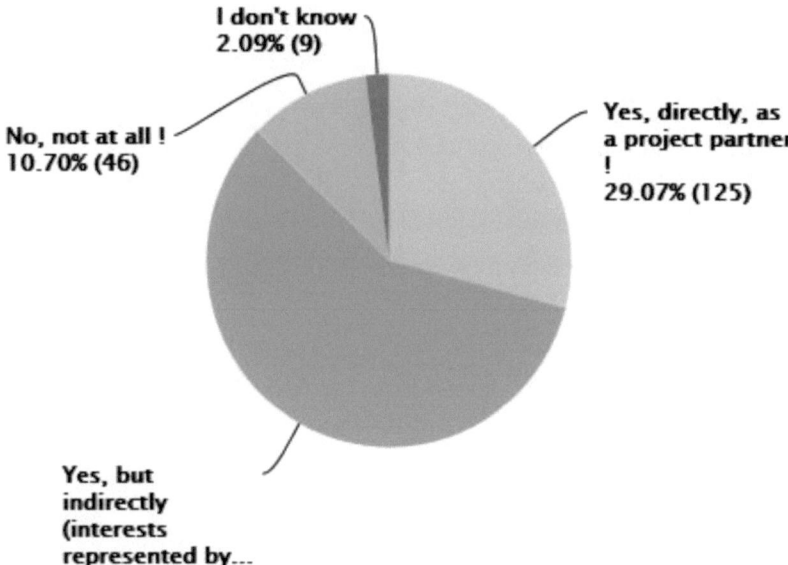

29 I   Participation of SMEs in project by different stakeholders

Remarkable is, that the number of universities suggesting a direct partnership is higher than rated by companies themselves.

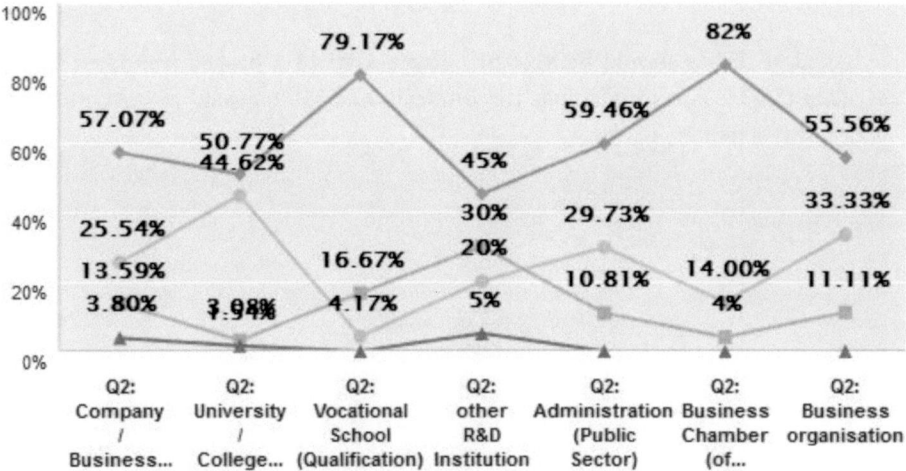

30 I   Reasons why few companies participate in projects

Even though it is possible for companies to become formal partners in some projects, the involvement of SMEs in EU funded projects is rather low. In the 7th Research Framework Programme only in 18 % of all projects including the private sector included a SME[20]. Given the huge numbers of SMEs that range around 99,2 % of all companies, this is a rather decent involvement. The participants were asked for the reasons, why so few companies join EU funded projects as partners and what the biggest hindrances might be.

The least challenge are the worries about Intellectual Property Rights (only 15,22 % marked this). In most EU funded projects, the results belong to the European Union and/or the public. It is often mentioned, that this hinders participation of companies, who are afraid to inform about their internal processes, share service or product ideas that will then be made available to their possible competitors.

Obviously the biggest problems concern the administrative burdens for companies (70,91 %, respectively 66,28 % also marked "complicated rules", a control question). SMEs simply lack the manpower and infrastructure needed to effectively implement projects. Unlike major companies, they do not have departments for accounting, project management etc. but often have to realise the project work besides their daily routine.

---

[20] http://ec.europa.eu/research/sme-techweb/pdf/sme_participaton_in_fp7_oct_2012_executive_summary.pdf

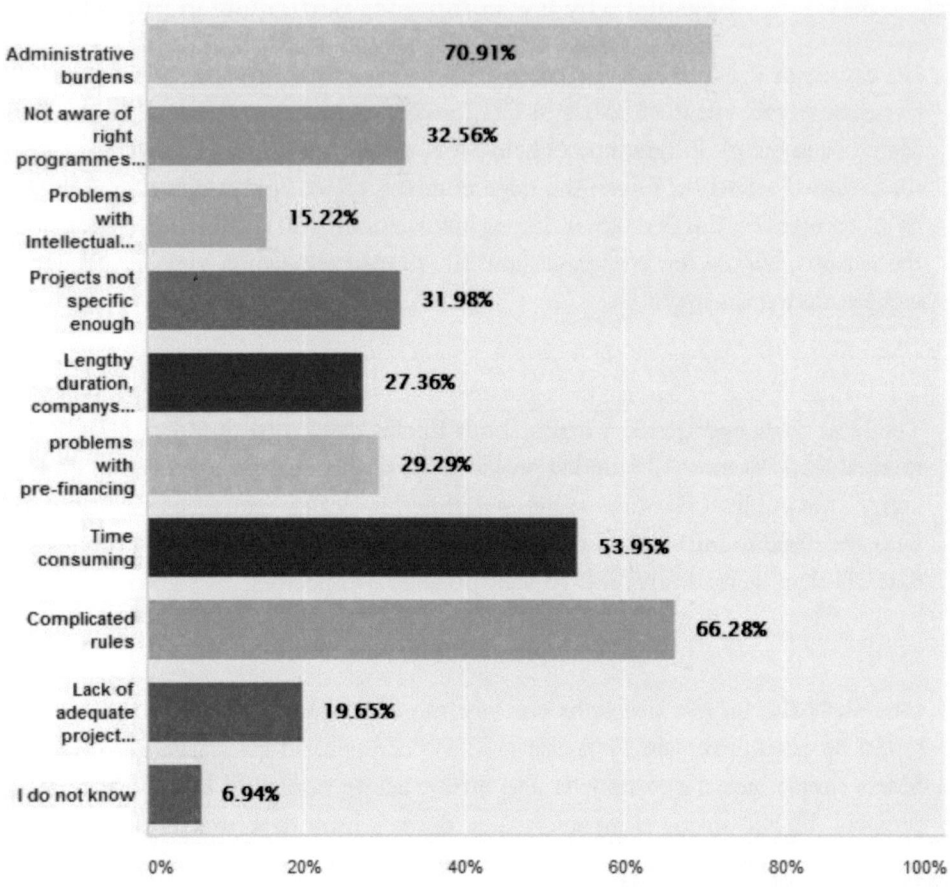

31 I   Why SMEs participate hardly in projects, answers from SMEs only

The result is quite identical, if the replies from SMEs are considered exclusively:

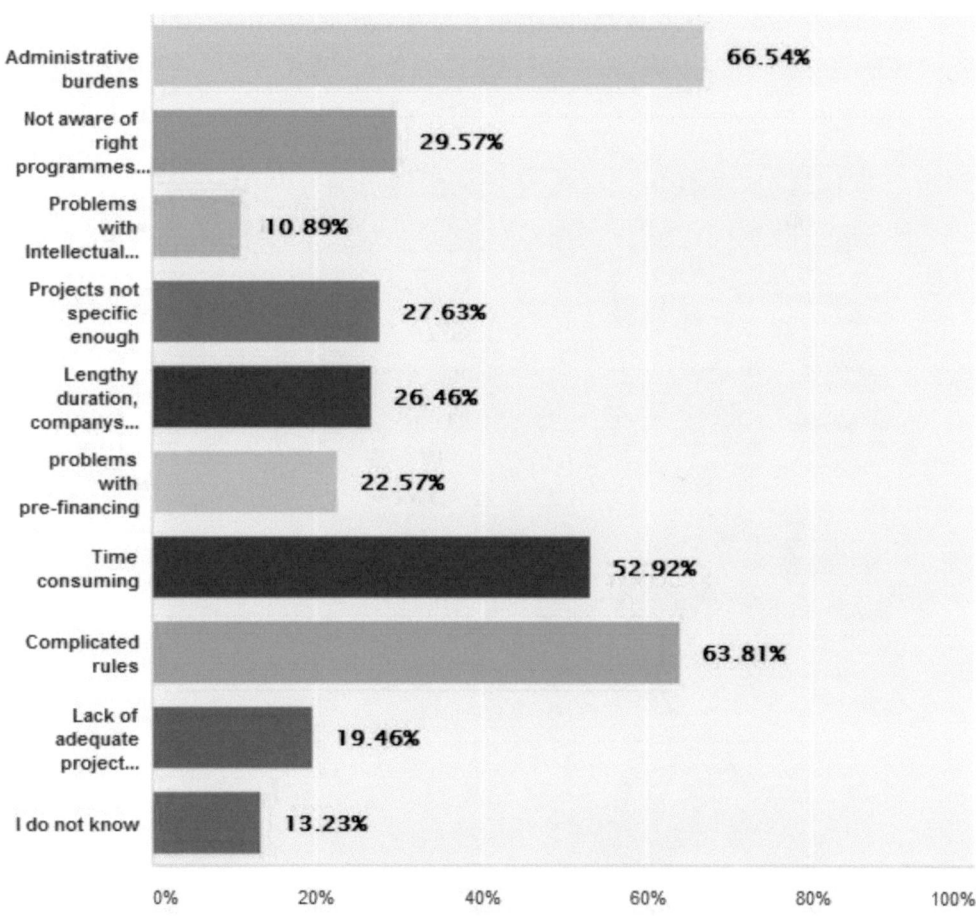

32 I   Important future sectors/topics for innovation in SMEs

Asked what kind of sector or topic the participants consider relevant when it comes to the innovation in SMEs in the future, the participants preferred Energy, Education and Soft Skills. At first this might be surprising, but considering the huge variety of SMEs (from bakeries to companies focusing on nanotechnology), these topics could be the common ground that affect all or most of companies. Despite from being a traditional craft company like carpenter or a firm developing lasers, all can benefit from energy savings, well-educated personnel and a high level of entrepreneurship.

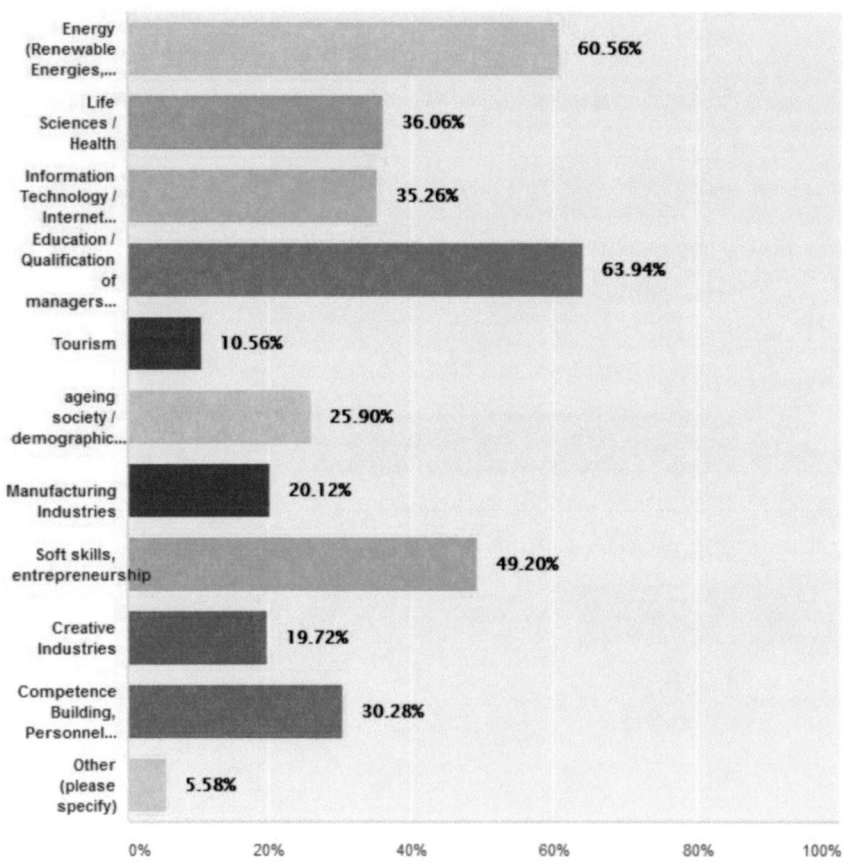

33 I by group of participants

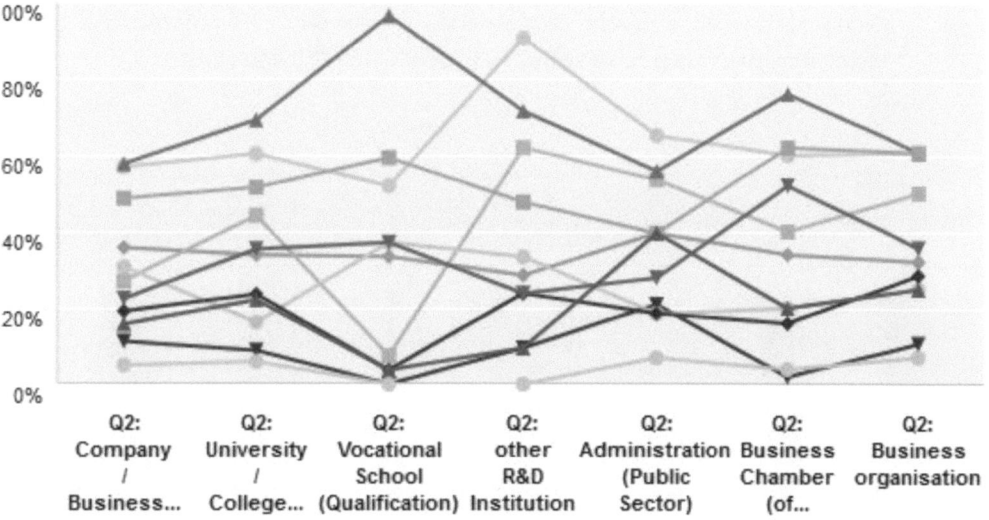

34 I   Cooperation for developing innovations

The surveyed were asked to indicate how important they consider a cooperation between SMEs and different organisations to develop innovations. The educational sector was mentioned most often, followed by R&D institutions.

	1 (not important)	2	3	4	5 (very important)	Total	Average Rating
Research institution (R&D)	8.98% 45	21.76% 109	18.16% 91	25.75% 129	25.35% 127	501	3.37
Public administration	26.49% 133	29.28% 147	25.50% 128	13.94% 70	4.78% 24	502	2.41
Educational institution (School, University)	1.00% 5	4.58% 23	14.54% 73	31.87% 160	48.01% 241	502	4.21
Business organisations/chambers	2.40% 12	9.40% 47	22.80% 114	36.80% 184	28.60% 143	500	3.80
International Cluster / Networks	8.38% 42	18.76% 94	27.15% 136	27.15% 136	18.56% 93	501	3.29
companies from same sector	10.93% 55	31.81% 160	27.04% 136	18.89% 95	11.33% 57	503	2.88
companies from different sectors	14.03% 70	31.26% 156	28.66% 143	15.03% 75	11.02% 55	499	2.78
Financial Institutions/Banks	38.05% 191	15.54% 78	16.53% 83	17.73% 89	12.15% 61	502	2.50
Private Consultants	56.80% 284	11% 55	15.40% 77	12.40% 62	4.40% 22	500	1.97

35 I   Biggest barriers for Innovation

Towards the end of the survey, the interviewed were asked to indicate the biggest barriers for innovation from their point of view. Again, it was not lack of finances at the top priority, but lack of qualified personnel and lack of management skills. This is a very frank and surprising result that could have been expected from public administrations and universities, but that companies also admit, that management lacks skill was not to be expected.

The overall biggest hindrance it the overall lack of qualified personnel and staff. Due to the demographic development in the Baltic Sea Region, this lack will even grow. There is a huge lack of young talents.

	1 (no problem)	2	3 (challenge)	4	5 (major problem)	Total	Average Rating
Lack of know-how, information	20.48% 102	22.69% 113	24.10% 120	14.26% 71	18.47% 92	498	2.88
Lack of qualified personnel/staff	2.20% 11	7.00% 35	17.60% 88	17.60% 88	55.60% 278	500	4.17
Financing	19.20% 96	20.80% 104	17.80% 89	19.20% 96	23% 115	500	3.06
Management lacks skills or expertise	1.82% 9	7.47% 37	18.18% 90	27.47% 136	45.05% 223	495	4.06
No international contacts	14.11% 69	24.95% 122	34.56% 169	18.20% 89	8.18% 40	489	2.81
Lack of entrepreneurship	5.87% 29	21.66% 107	36.64% 181	23.28% 115	12.55% 62	494	3.15
No access to R&D	15.24% 75	27.44% 135	30.69% 151	20.73% 102	5.89% 29	492	2.75
Lack of time	21.50% 106	24.34% 120	23.73% 117	18.26% 90	12.17% 60	493	2.75
Administrative rules, complex public procurement	48.48% 239	12.78% 63	13.18% 65	16.23% 80	9.33% 46	493	2.25
Lack of vision, motivation	30.91% 153	23.43% 116	22.02% 109	13.33% 66	10.30% 51	495	2.49
Risk (uncertain if innovation fits market)	31.12% 155	20.48% 102	24.90% 124	14.26% 71	9.24% 46	498	2.50
no awareness (why innovation is necessary)	8.31% 25	14.62% 44	24.25% 73	20.93% 63	31.89% 96	301	3.53

sorted by professional background

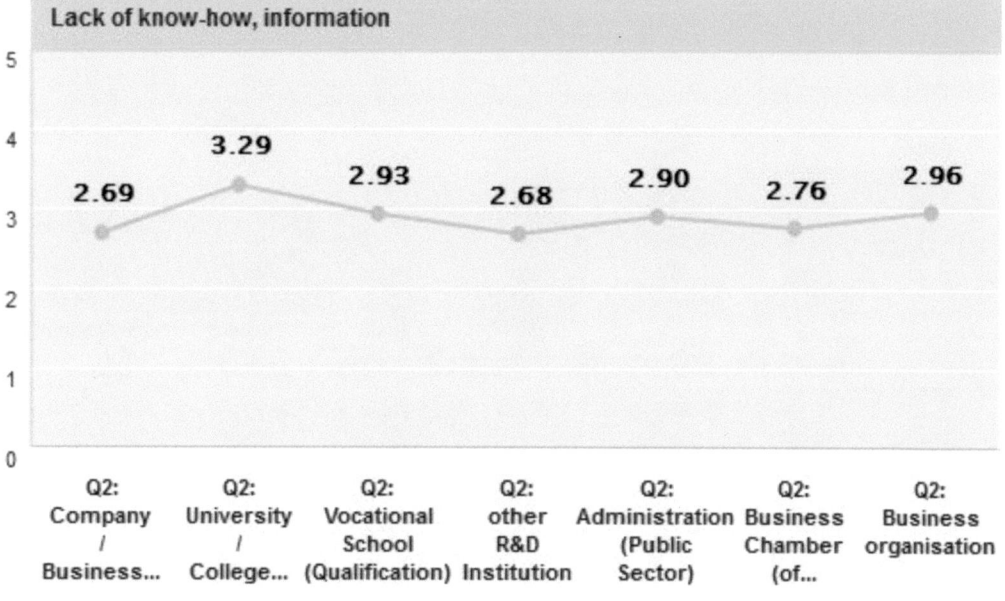

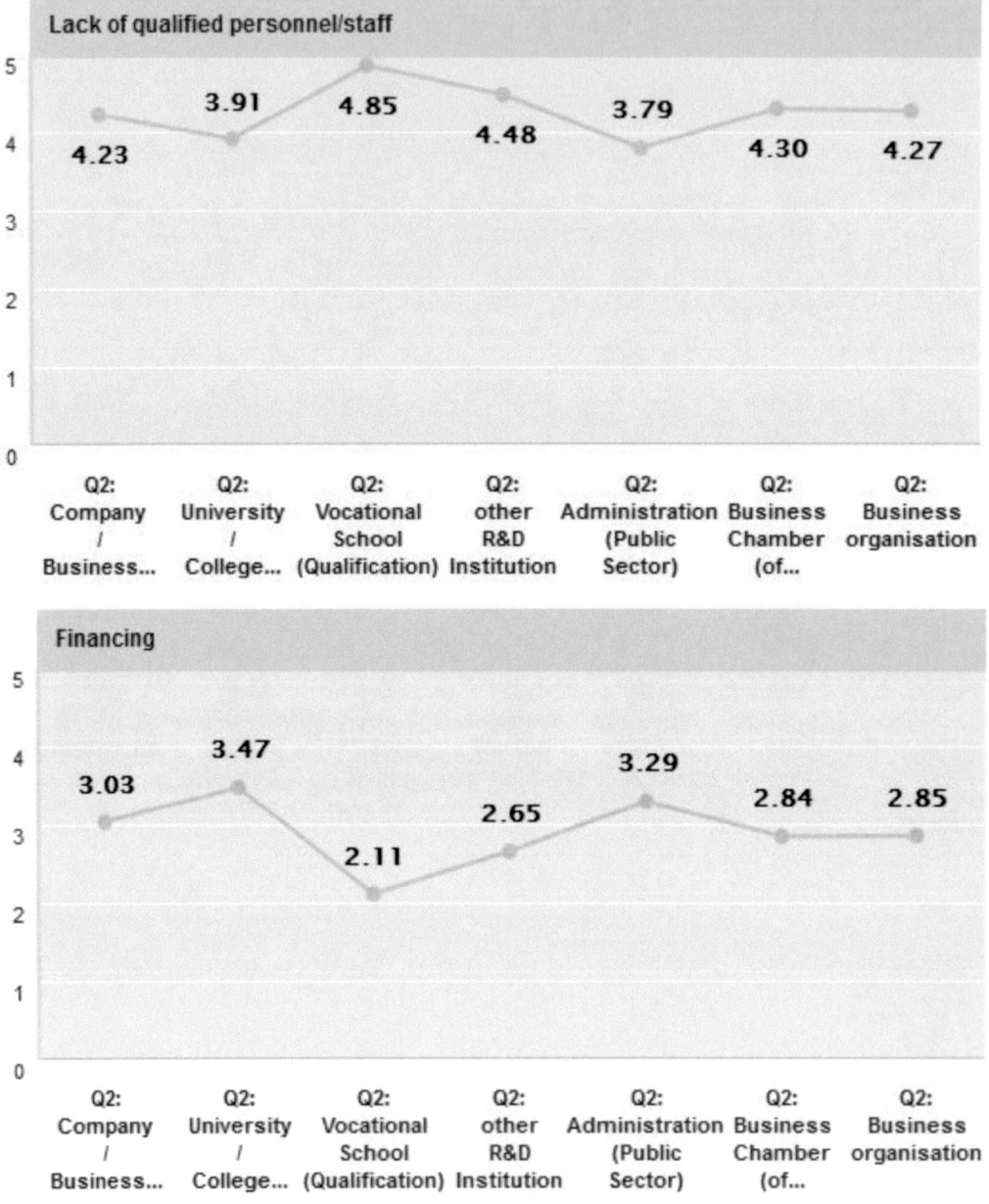

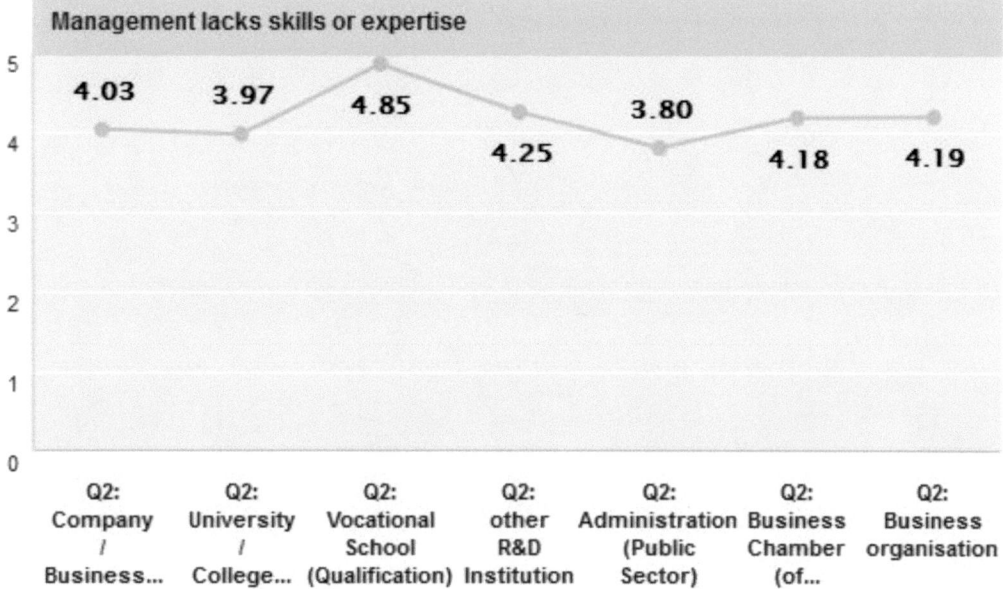

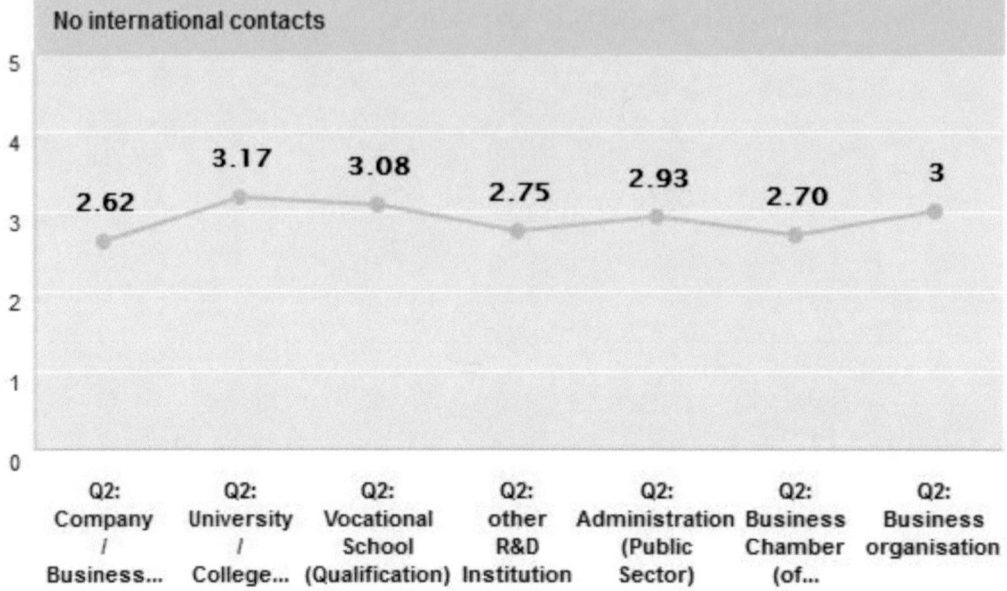

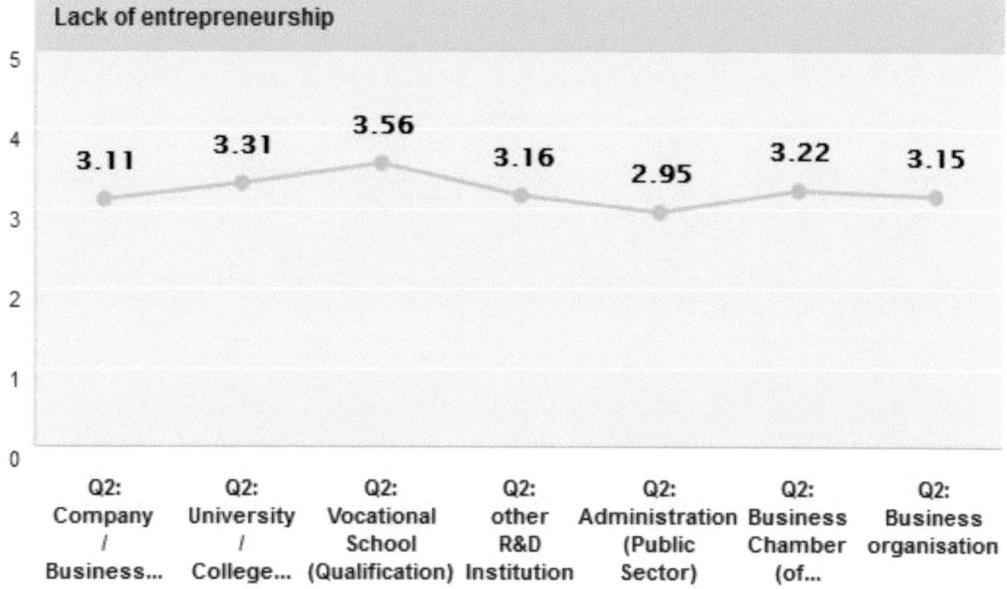

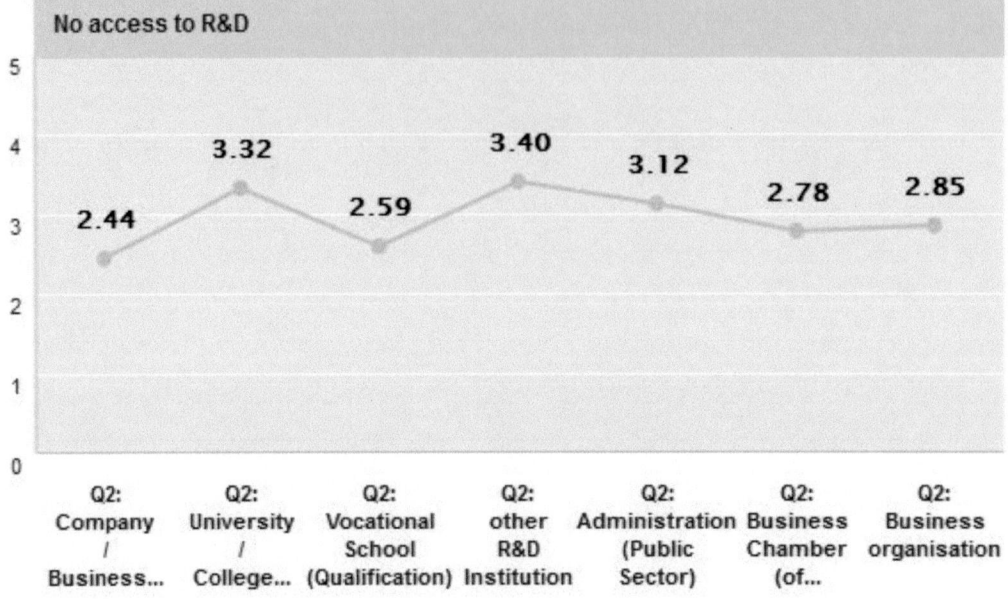

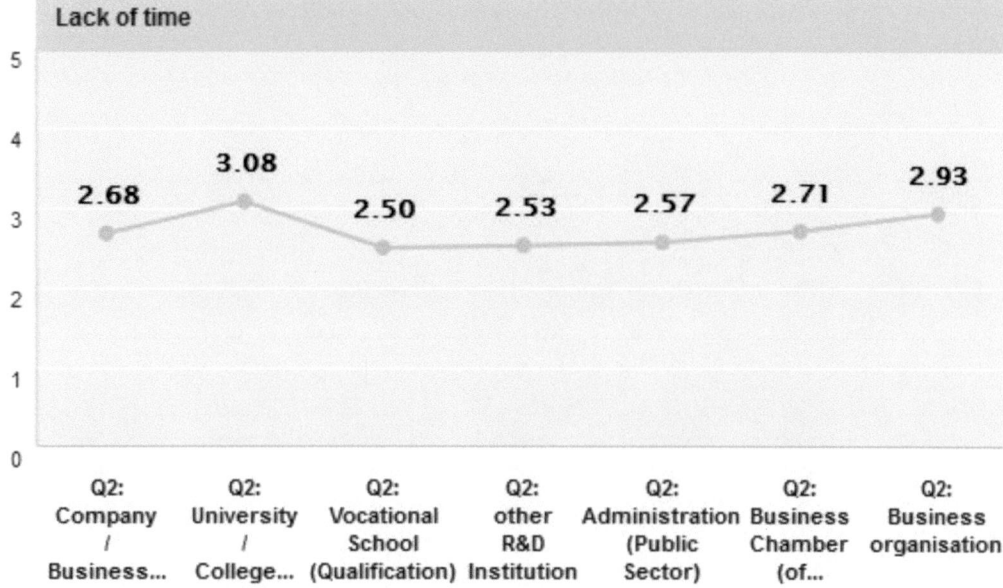

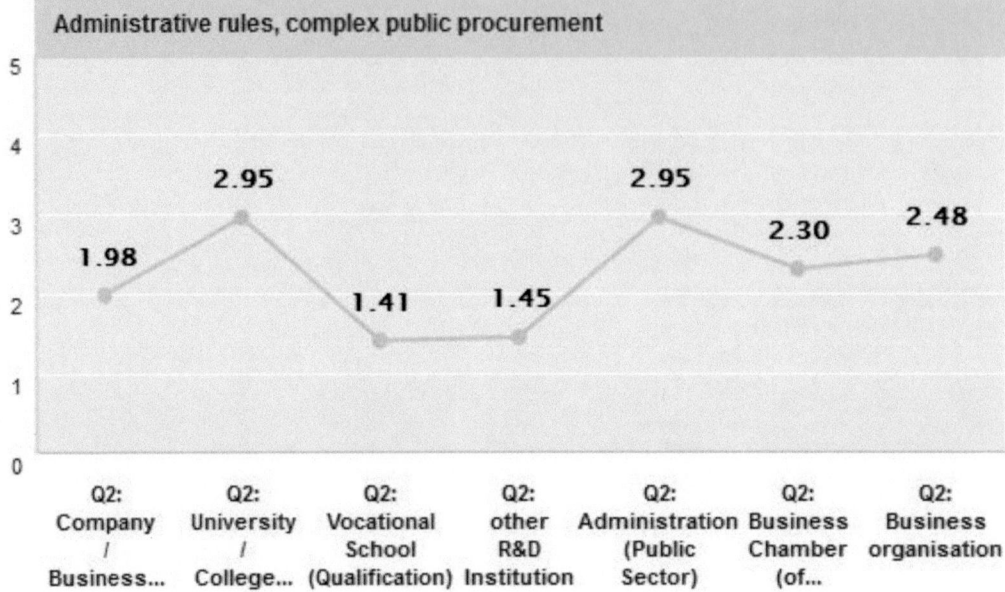

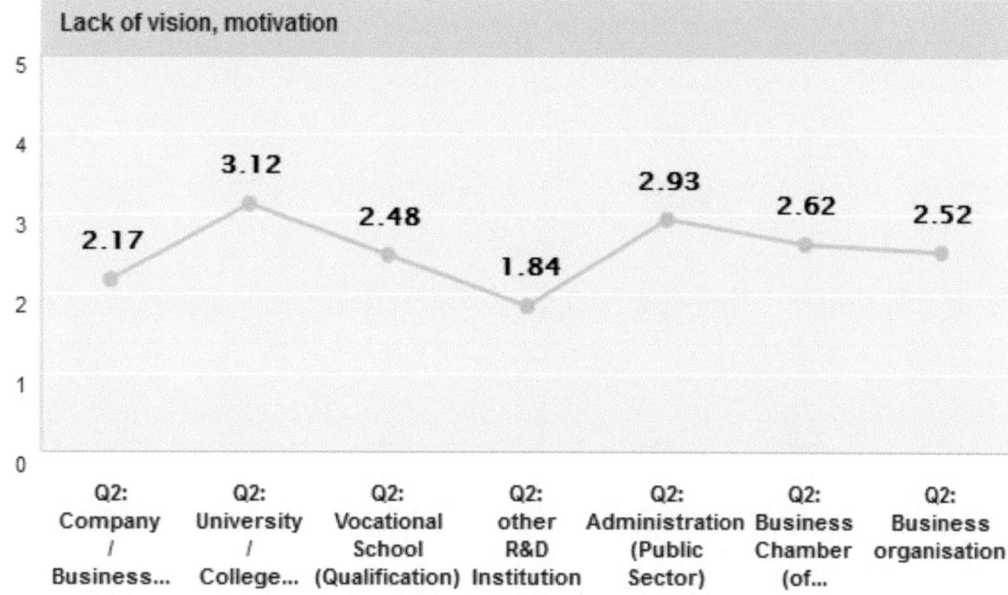

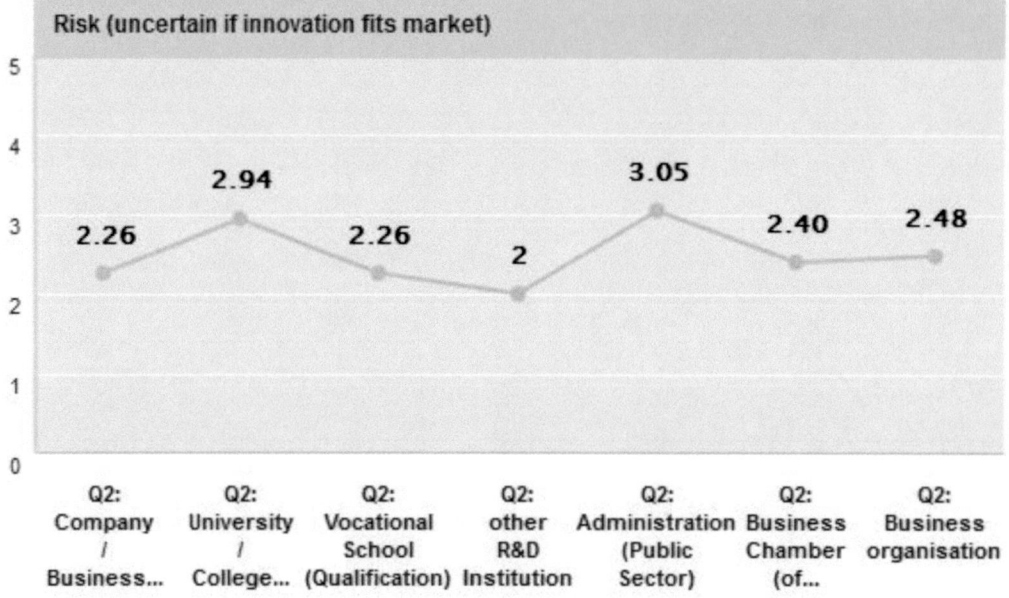

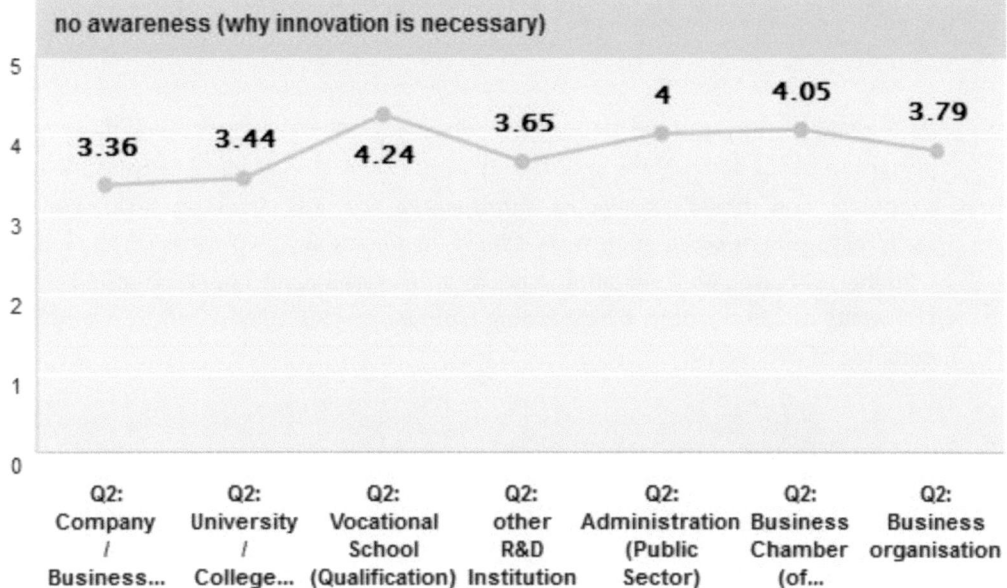

36 I   Support to increase innovation in SMEs

At the end of the surveyed were asked, what very general support they think is important to foster innovations in SMEs. It was evident, that political support, financial support   and better access to information are less relevant, than qualified staff/management and a good work climate in a company. To focus on the internal working processes, an innovation friendly work climate, an approach tested by the University of Lund within a long lasting national project called Kraft, is a surprising outcome of the survey.

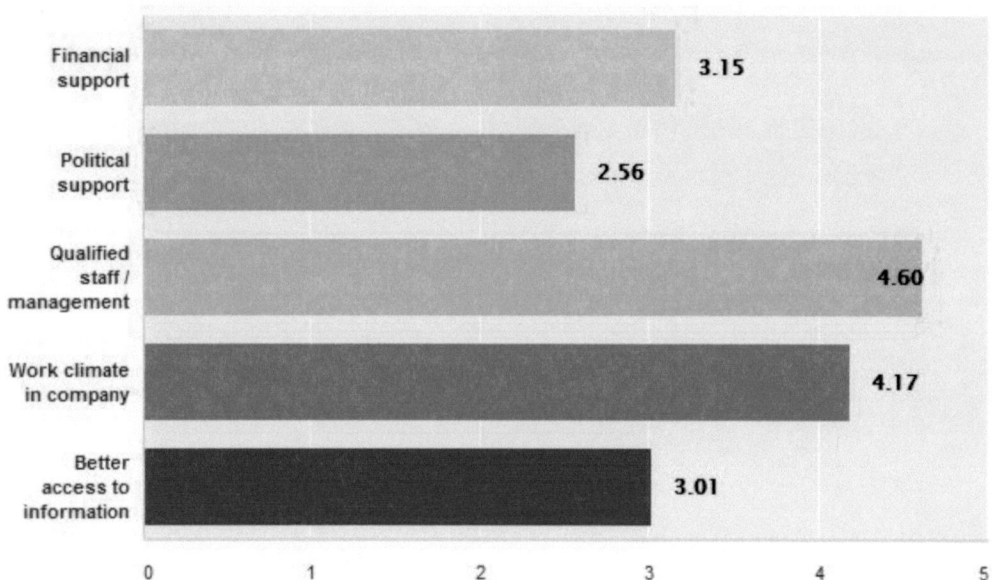

	not relevant	(no label)	(no label)	(no label)	very important	Total	Average Rating
Financial support	17.06% 87	24.51% 125	12.55% 64	18.43% 94	27.45% 140	510	3.15
Political support	25.39% 129	30.91% 157	18.31% 93	13.19% 67	12.20% 62	508	2.56
Qualified staff / management	0.20% 1	0.99% 5	8.09% 41	19.72% 100	71.01% 360	507	4.60
Work climate in company	1.38% 7	4.54% 23	16.17% 82	31.36% 159	46.55% 236	507	4.17
Better access to information	18.15% 92	19.33% 98	22.29% 113	24.26% 123	15.98% 81	507	3.01

sorted by group of participants

The results of the respective groups confirms the average outcome to a large extent. No matter of the professional background, all respondents marked qualified staff/management with the highest priority, followed by work climate.

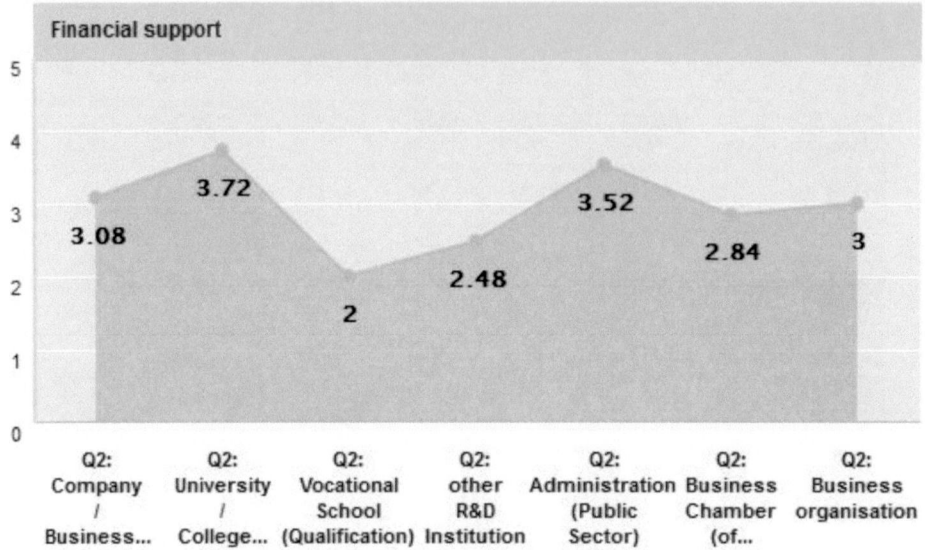

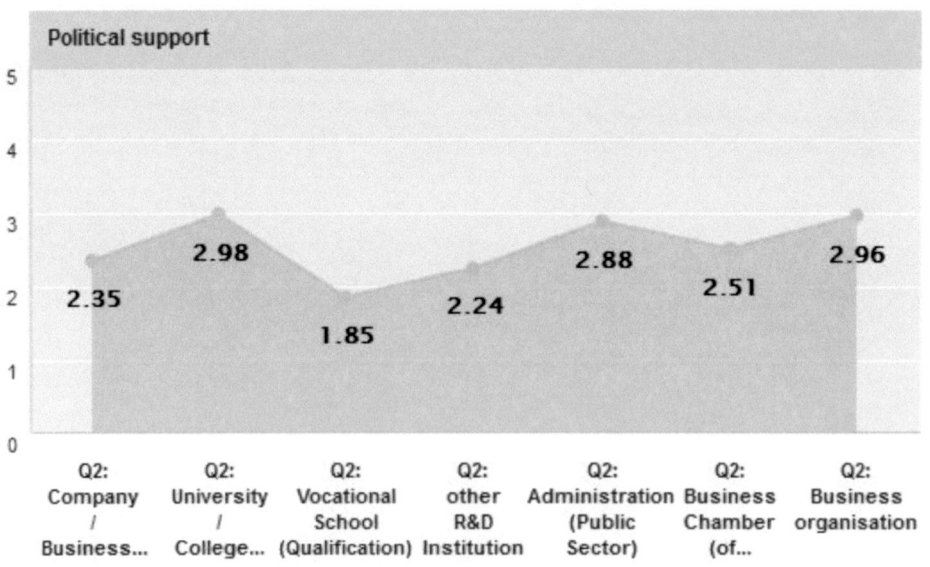

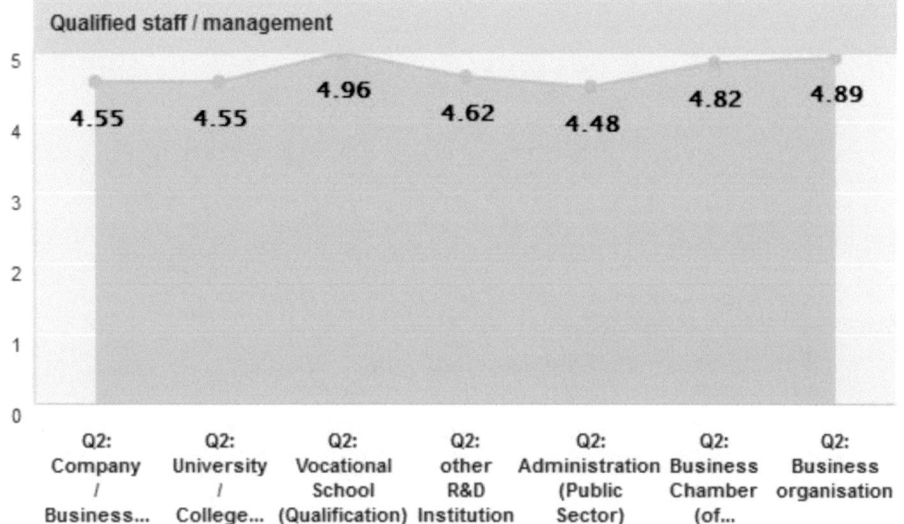

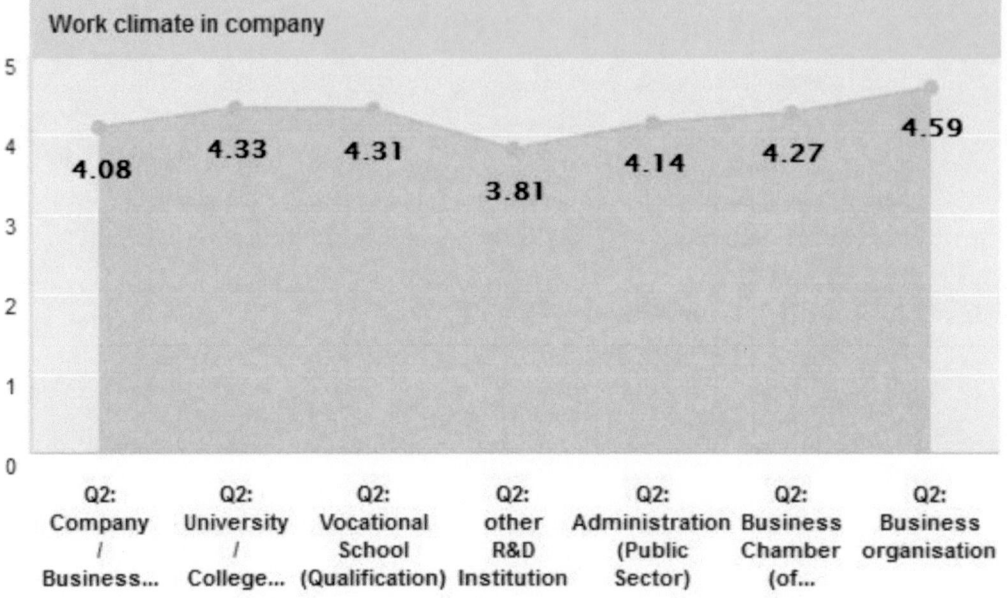

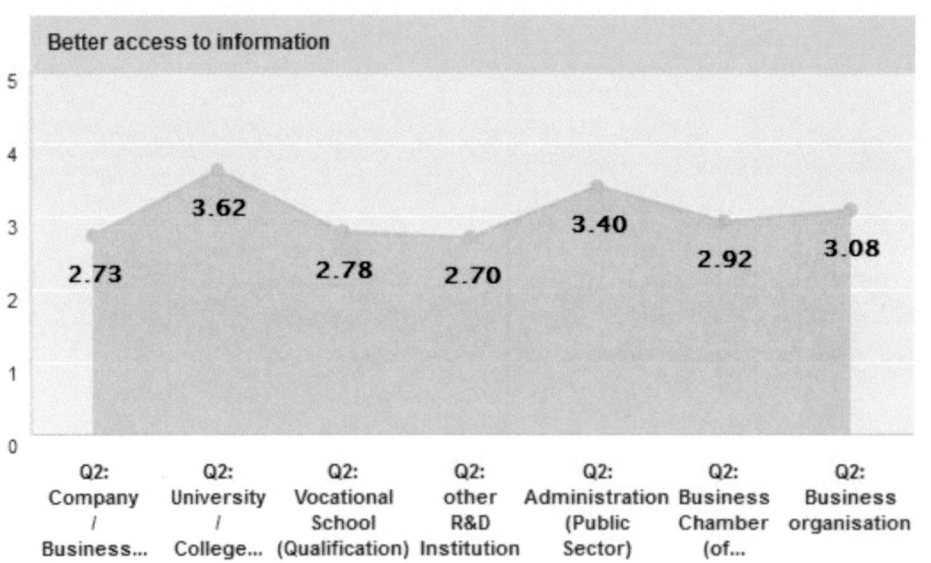

37 I   Conclusions

When it comes to innovation in SMEs, the Baltic Sea Region seems to be divided in Northern regions and Southern regions. It is evident, that companies from some countries, in particular northern regions like Sweden (91,84 %) or Denmark (90 %) consider themselves much more innovative, than southern countries like Poland (43,33 %) or Russia (34,78 %). This might indicate also a different self-confidence of the entrepreneurs in the respective countries.

Most innovative companies are currently focusing on product innovations. The rather less well-known organizational innovations, the way companies work, internal coop- eration between employees, methods like lean management etc. are hardly exploited. Here the biggest gaps are evident, for example very low levels in countries with a traditional hierarchic, top-to-bottom structure, like Belarus, Poland and Russia, while a much higher level of these innovations exists in Sweden or Norway with a higher level of cooperation among employees and managers.

Almost all companies believe, that innovations are essential to stay competitive (78,28%).

It is clear from the survey that innovative companies are active on bigger markets, either national or even international. In this context, it can be assumed, that either international contacts help companies to become or stay innovative or that already innovative companies find it easier to expand their businesses.

The survey confirms, that most companies are not engaged in R&D of their own, in particular the micro and small companies. These companies, that represent the major- ity of all businesses, lack the manpower to have R&D Departments. They rely on networking and external R&D solutions, like cooperating with other companies or organisations. Those few companies that are engaged in R&D activities invest quite a lot of their own budget for research and development tasks, in average between 10-15 %.

Other than companies, the highest innovation level is among R&D institutes and Universities in the Baltic Sea Region.

With regards to innovation in SMEs, the key to a successful promotion lies within the on-going cooperation with between the companies and the supporting organisations. In this context, vocational schools, qualifying personnel for SMEs in 2 – 3 years, indicated the highest level of cooperation with SMEs, followed by Chamber of Commerce and Craft and other Business Organisations. R&D Institutes and public administrations indicated a rather low level of cooperation with SMEs.

Innovative companies are fully aware of the advantages of SMEs more than non-innovative companies, i.e. fast-decision making, low hierarchy, customer-focus. It has been mentioned, that these often stated advantages are right, but some SMEs need to become aware of them and not consider them as a disadvantage, e.g. being small can be an advantage compared to major industries who are not flexible at all.

Asked what future innovations are needed, a surprisingly high level indicated that process and organizational innovations are almost as important as product innovations. Examining the answers per country, show that product innovations are much more asked for in countries like Belarus, Poland and Russia. Nordic countries like Denmark, Norway and Sweden expressed a much higher interest in process/service and organizational innovations in SMEs. As it has been confirmed in the comments to this questions, these soft innovations embody the biggest potentials for the Baltic Sea Region, since they are open to any companies, independent from the specific services or products they might offer.

Inquired if companies should be able to become formal partners in project, the result is surprising. Only 29,07 % suggest SMEs becoming formal partners. With 58,14 %

the majority of respondents recommends that the interest of SMEs need to be represented by umbrella organisation. Only 10.7 % would not like to see SMEs in innovation projects at all. It has been commented, that the results are important. SMEs need to benefit from projects, which is not bound to being a partner or not. Almost all surveyed believe, that the administrative workload is too much for SMEs, keeping them from wanting to be a partner.

When it comes to important future sectors for innovation in SMEs, the participants preferred Energy, Education and Soft Skills. At first this might be surprising, but considering the huge variety of SMEs (from bakeries to companies focusing on nano-technology), these topics could be the common ground that affect all or most of companies. Despite from being a traditional craft company like carpenter or a firm developing lasers, all can benefit from energy savings, well-educated personnel and a high level of entrepreneurship.

Cooperation is considered very important to develop innovative solutions in SMEs. Most important is a close cooperation with educational institutes, followed by business organisations and chambers that can function as multipliers and facilitators. A cooperation with banks and private consultants is not considered important.

The biggest hindrances for effective innovation in SMEs is by far the lack of adequate skilled workforce and the qualification level of managers . Secondly, entrepreneurship and lack of awareness why innovations are important to companies were mentioned.

Innovative companies do not consider help from the outside in form of financial support as important as non-innovative companies. All companies identify the lack of skilled workforce and adequate qualifications as one of the biggest hindrances to allow innovations in companies.

The attraction of adequate personnel and better qualified managers seems to be the bottleneck for developments of innovative companies.

The comments at the end of the survey confirmed once again, that the attraction of talents and development of non-technological innovations will be one of the biggest challenges for innovative SMEs in the future innovations in SMEs in the Baltic Sea Region.

3. Part – Action Fields

A short-term innovation support for SMEs can hardly achieve great success. It must rather be implemented reliably in the long term. The development of the cooperation structures and the involvement of the SMEs takes time, so that a progressive development with continuous growth of the participating SMEs is crucial.

The Baltic Region has been historically one of the most innovative regions in the world and has also today many innovation potentials that need to be exploited. The growing international competition can only be mastered, if the Baltic Sea Region is faster and better than other regions and will once again be one of the most innovative regions. A highly qualified population is a prerequisite.

The Baltic Sea region has centers and regions with very high innovative strengths; there is a lot of catching up in other regions. These regions need to be aligned. An enhanced innovation in rural areas is needed; the different rural areas need to be better connected to the urban research- and development capacities. Effective innovation strategies in the Baltic Sea region must build on the region-specific strengths and use the cultural differences as a creative source.

In accordance with the economic and social importance of small- and medium-sized enterprises and to use the excellent future prospects of the SMEs of the Baltic Sea region the following three action fields need the most attention in the next years:

1 I Education, vocational training and talents

In the long run, the innovation level of a region corresponds to the level of qualifications. The best promotion is one that targets the education of future entrepreneurs and employees. The survey 2013 clearly showed that a lack of skilled workforce is considered the biggest hindrance for innovation in SMEs. In almost all BSR countries the number of people of working age will decline by up to 20% in the next 15 years. More work based learning is needed.

Therefore it is essential to exploit the full human potential and develop qualifications fitting SMEs, i.e. by

- focusing on entrepreneurship
- establishing qualifications that correspond to the practical needs of SMEs by combining vocational training and academic education (like in the Dual System that proved highly effective in Finland and Germany)
- fostering high potentials, but also weaker learners, fighting youth unemployment and thus counteract the growing lack of workforce
- Mobility is also critical for future employees of innovative SMEs
- More educational facilities in the Baltic Sea Region, universities but also vocational schools, should actively promote the exchange of students and in particular of trainees

Highly qualified personnel are the prerequisite for any innovative company and must be the highest priority. Investments in the required qualifications pay the best interest rates and are the best method for a sustainable promotion of innovations!

2 I SME infrastructure and cooperation

The evaluation of the projects and the survey both confirmed that the innovation level of a company directly corresponds to its level of networking and cooperation.

There is also a strong correlation between the level of international activity of SMEs and innovation. Small firms lack own R&D departments and manpower to be innovative – they need external resources:

- Networks driven by business organisations representing the needs of SMEs and collecting their input must be strengthened and connected to academic networks
- Demand-driven research resulting in short terms in applied knowledge for companies must be a target
- The collaboration of SMEs and universities must be greatly improved to develop tangible, innovative solutions for individual companies or groups of enterprises in their regions and on a transnational level.
- SMEs need also to cooperate strongly with each other, the transfer of best practices between companies needs to be supported.

Such a specific infrastructure for the support of innovation in SMEs should be based on the integration of already existing organisations, whose capacities, experience and long lasting contacts with SMEs are a sound basis. The regional disparities in innovation performance need to be considered. Using and pooling existing resources reduces costs, saves time and ensures success in the long run. Networks need to be built on the respective regional strengths and connected on a trans regional level in the Baltic Sea Region, bringing smart specialisation to its true meaning.

3 I More than one innovation

Innovations are more than pure product developments and new technologies. Especially in SMEs innovations do ask for a comprehensive understanding of the unique possibilities and potentials of the companies. Only very few companies are innovating from within, without using external resources; most companies need to open up and become part of the emerging "open innovations" environments. Different kinds of innovation must be considered:

- **Product innovations** need to be based on customer needs, and SMEs need support in polishing their product innovations for market introduction.
- **Process innovations** refer to a new or significantly improved production process, distribution method, marketing or support activity for goods or services.
- **Social and organisational innovations** refer to the way the staff works together in a company, the internal work climate, or innovative thinking and leading of the managers.

An innovation can be seen as the implementation of a new or significantly improved product (good or service), or process, a new marketing method, or a new organisational method in business practices, workplace organisation or external relations. However, most innovations today concentrate heavily on product innovations, while the potential of process innovations remains untapped.

The survey 2013 showed that in particular non-technological innovations, like social and organisational innovations, are of high priority for SMEs, yet the funding programmes focus on the promotion of product innovations only. Support in the area of non-technological innovations forms an essential basis for all subsequent changes and therefore must be treated with at least equal attention as technical innovation support measures.